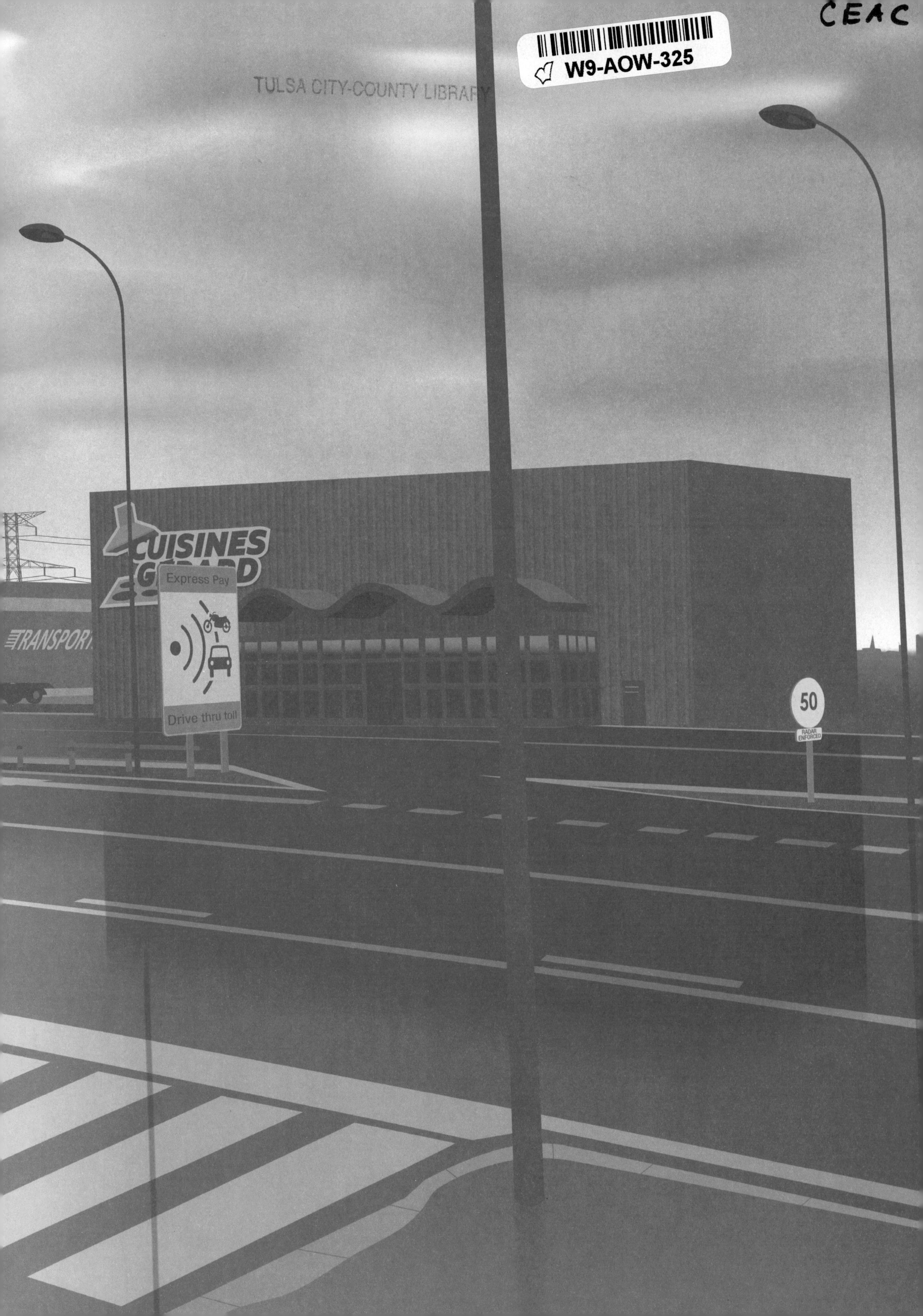
CUISINES
Express Pay
Drive thru toll
TRANSPORT
50
RADAR ENFORCED

ARTHUR DE PINS

Zombillenium

3. Control Freaks

NANTIER • BEALL • MINOUSTCHINE
Publishing inc.
new york

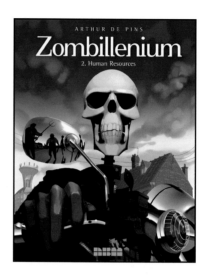

Also available:
Zombillenium, vols.1, 2 $14.99 each

SEE MORE AND ORDER AT NBMPUB.COM
AND CHECK OUT ZOMBILLENIUM. COM

We have over 200 titles available
NBM
160 Broadway, Suite 700, East Wing
New York, NY 10038
Catalog available by request
If ordering by mail add $4 P&H 1st item, $1 each addt'l

Due to my strong personal convictions,
I wish to stress that this comic in no way
endorses a belief in social dumping

ARTHUR DE PINS

ISBN 9781561639564
© DUPUIS 2013, by De Pins
www.dupuis.com
All rights reserved.
Library of Congress Control Number 2015939367

Printed in China
First printing August 2015

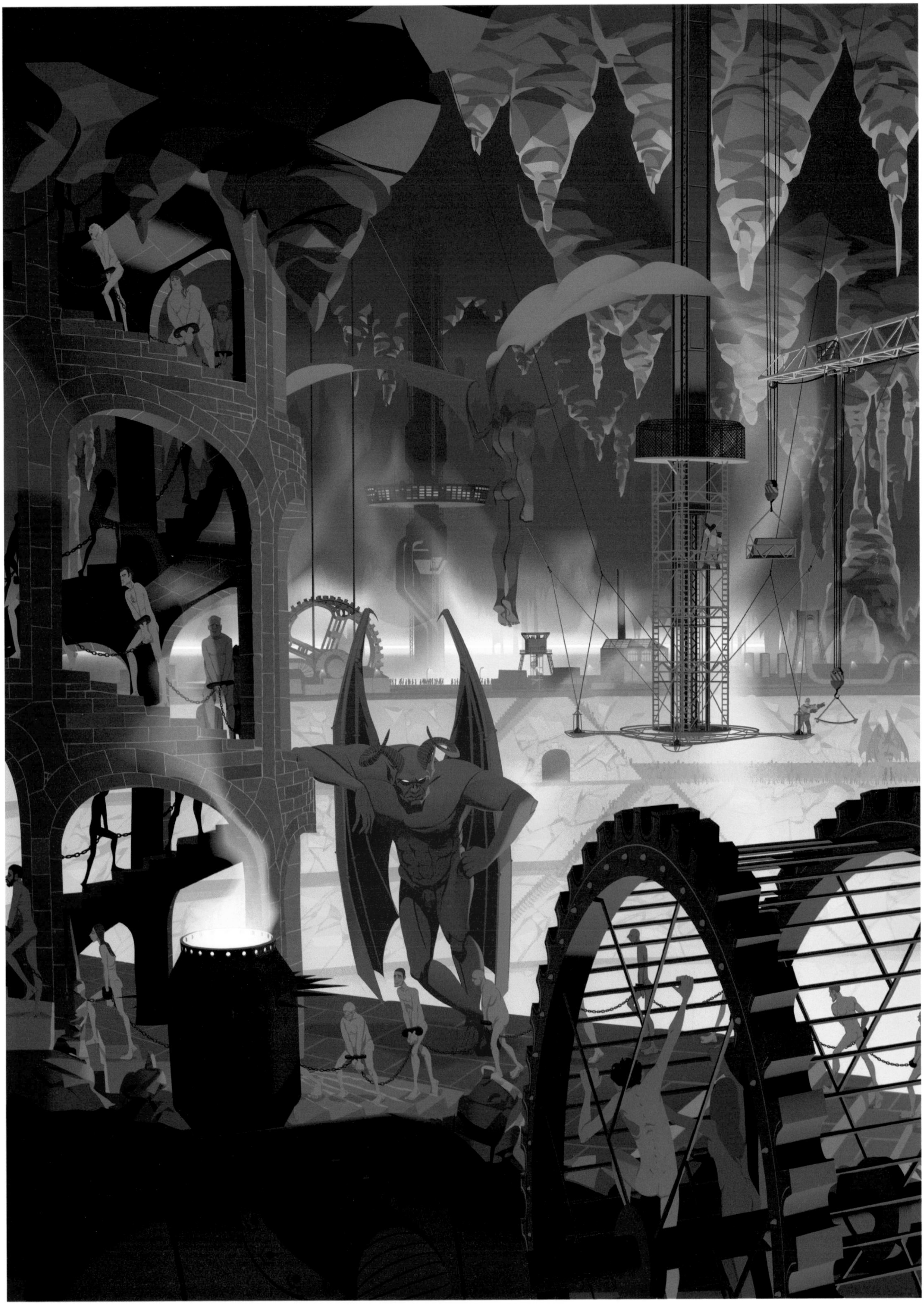

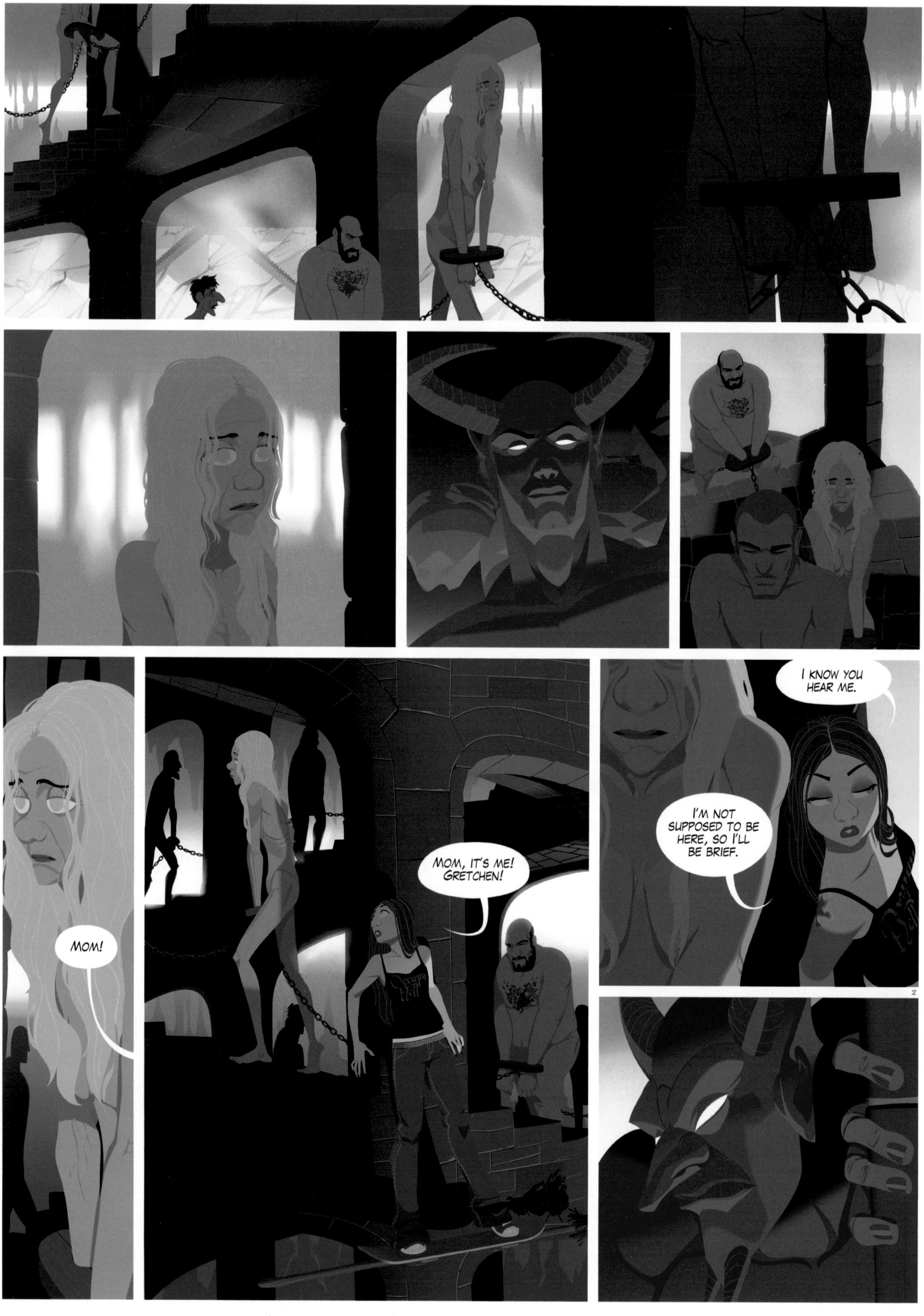
MOM!
MOM, IT'S ME! GRETCHEN!
I KNOW YOU HEAR ME.
I'M NOT SUPPOSED TO BE HERE, SO I'LL BE BRIEF.

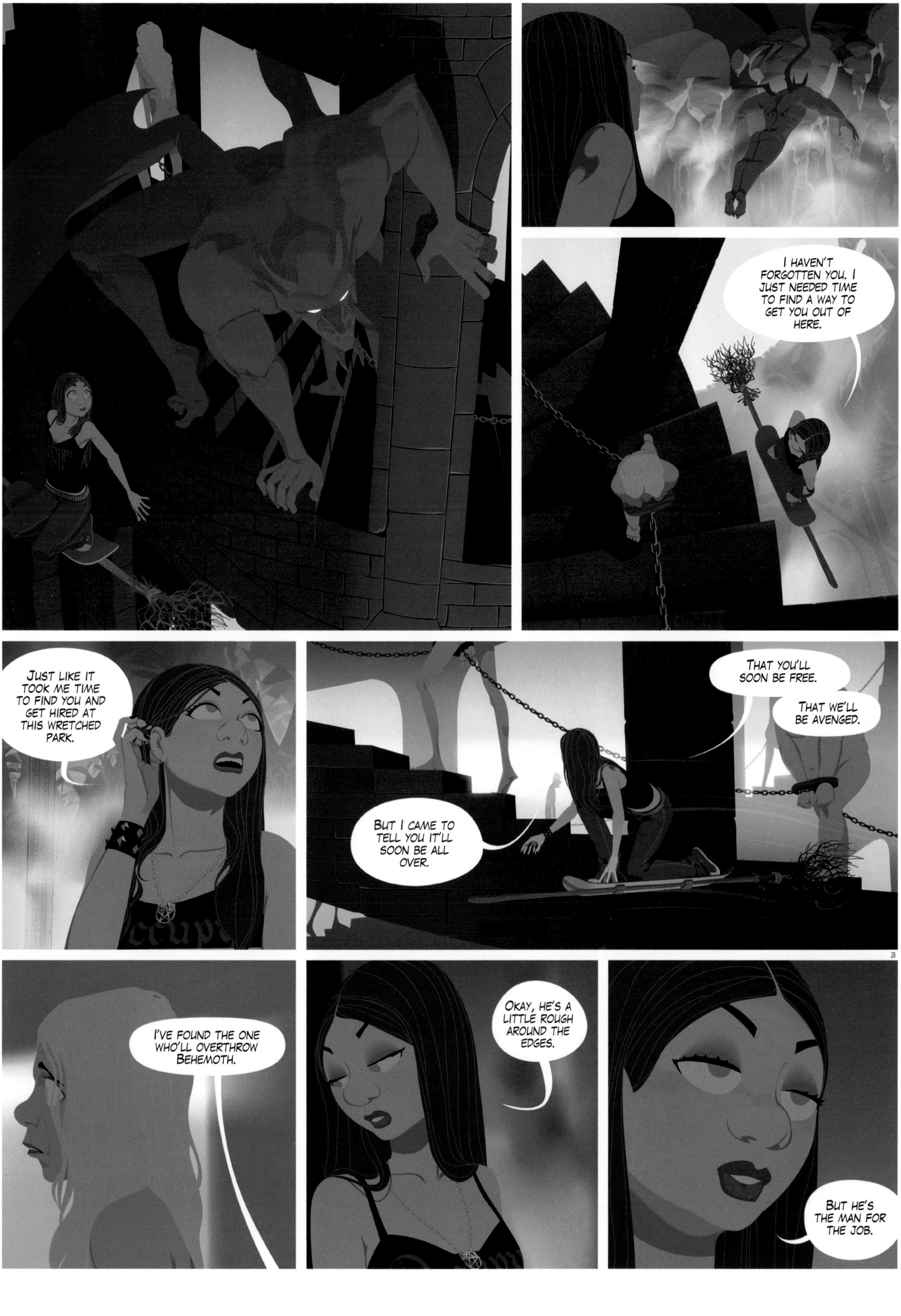
I HAVEN'T FORGOTTEN YOU. I JUST NEEDED TIME TO FIND A WAY TO GET YOU OUT OF HERE.
JUST LIKE IT TOOK ME TIME TO FIND YOU AND GET HIRED AT THIS WRETCHED PARK.
BUT I CAME TO TELL YOU IT'LL SOON BE ALL OVER.
THAT YOU'LL SOON BE FREE.
THAT WE'LL BE AVENGED.
I'VE FOUND THE ONE WHO'LL OVERTHROW BEHEMOTH.
OKAY, HE'S A LITTLE ROUGH AROUND THE EDGES.
BUT HE'S THE MAN FOR THE JOB.

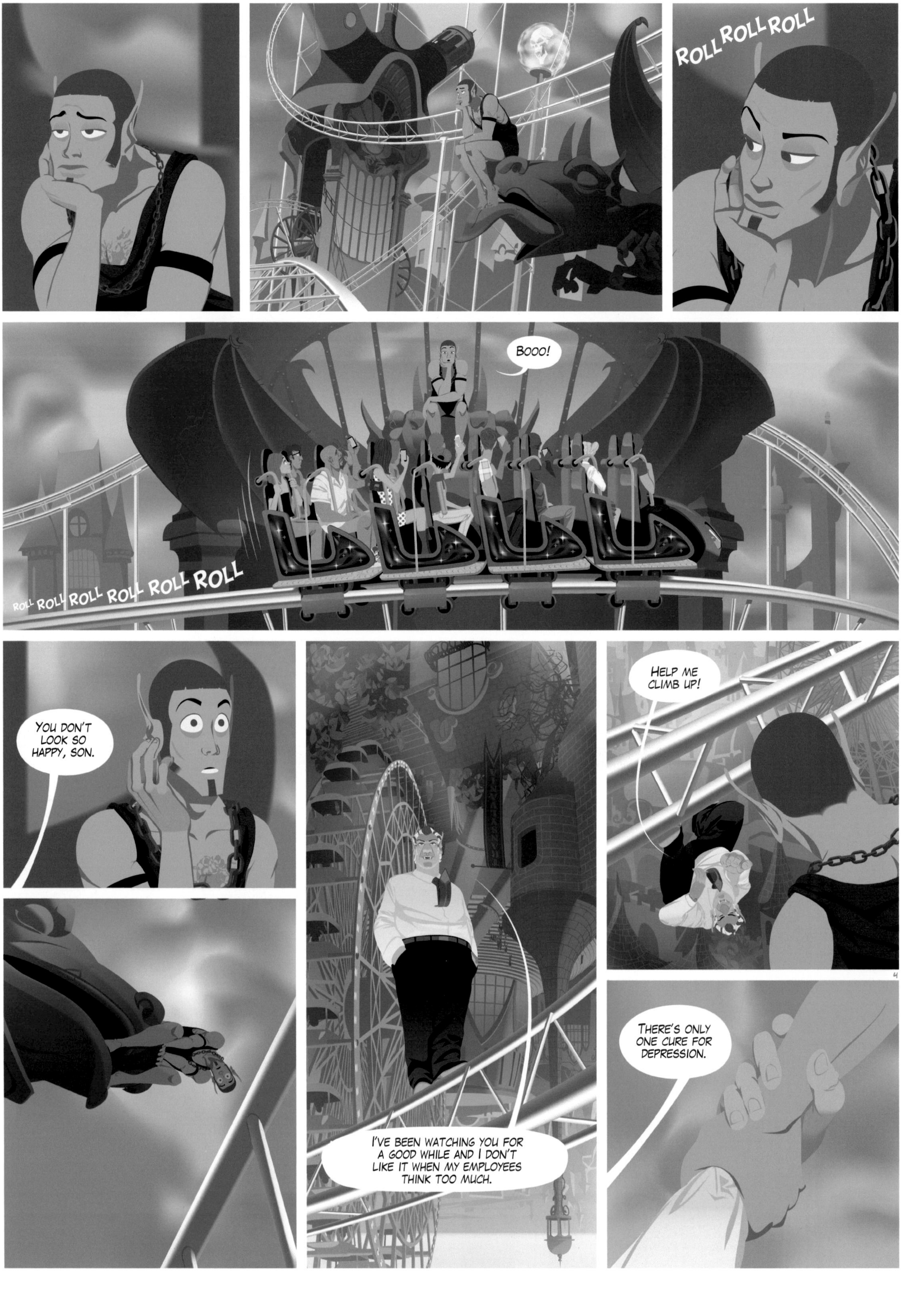
ROLL ROLL ROLL
BOOO!
ROLL ROLL ROLL ROLL ROLL ROLL
YOU DON'T LOOK SO HAPPY, SON.
I'VE BEEN WATCHING YOU FOR A GOOD WHILE AND I DON'T LIKE IT WHEN MY EMPLOYEES THINK TOO MUCH.
HELP ME CLIMB UP!
THERE'S ONLY ONE CURE FOR DEPRESSION.

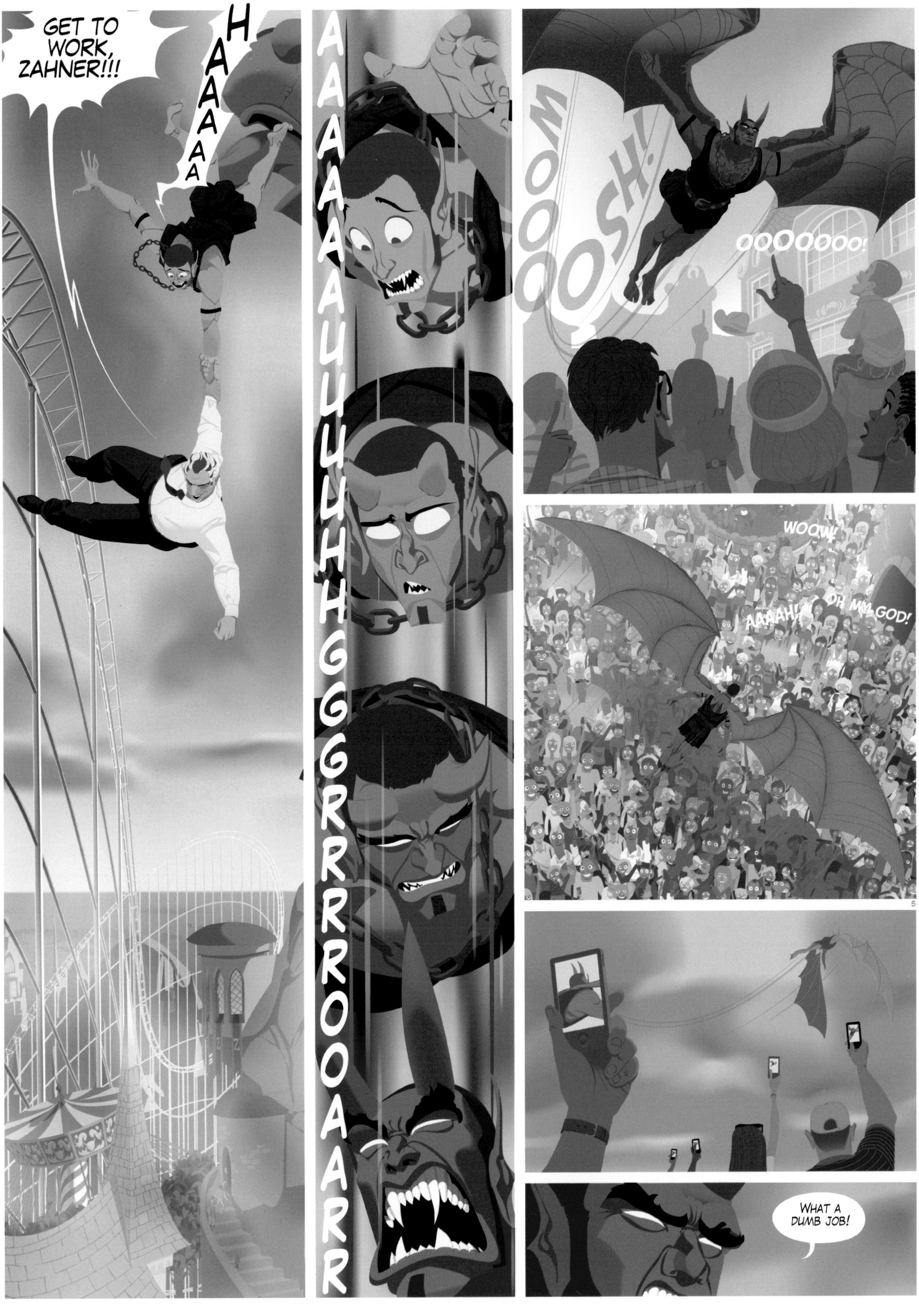
GET TO WORK, ZAHNER!!!
HAAAAAA
AAAAAAAUUUUHHGGGRRRRROOOAARR
WOOOOOSH!
oOOOOoo!
WOOW!
AAAAH!
OH MY GOD!
WHAT A DUMB JOB!

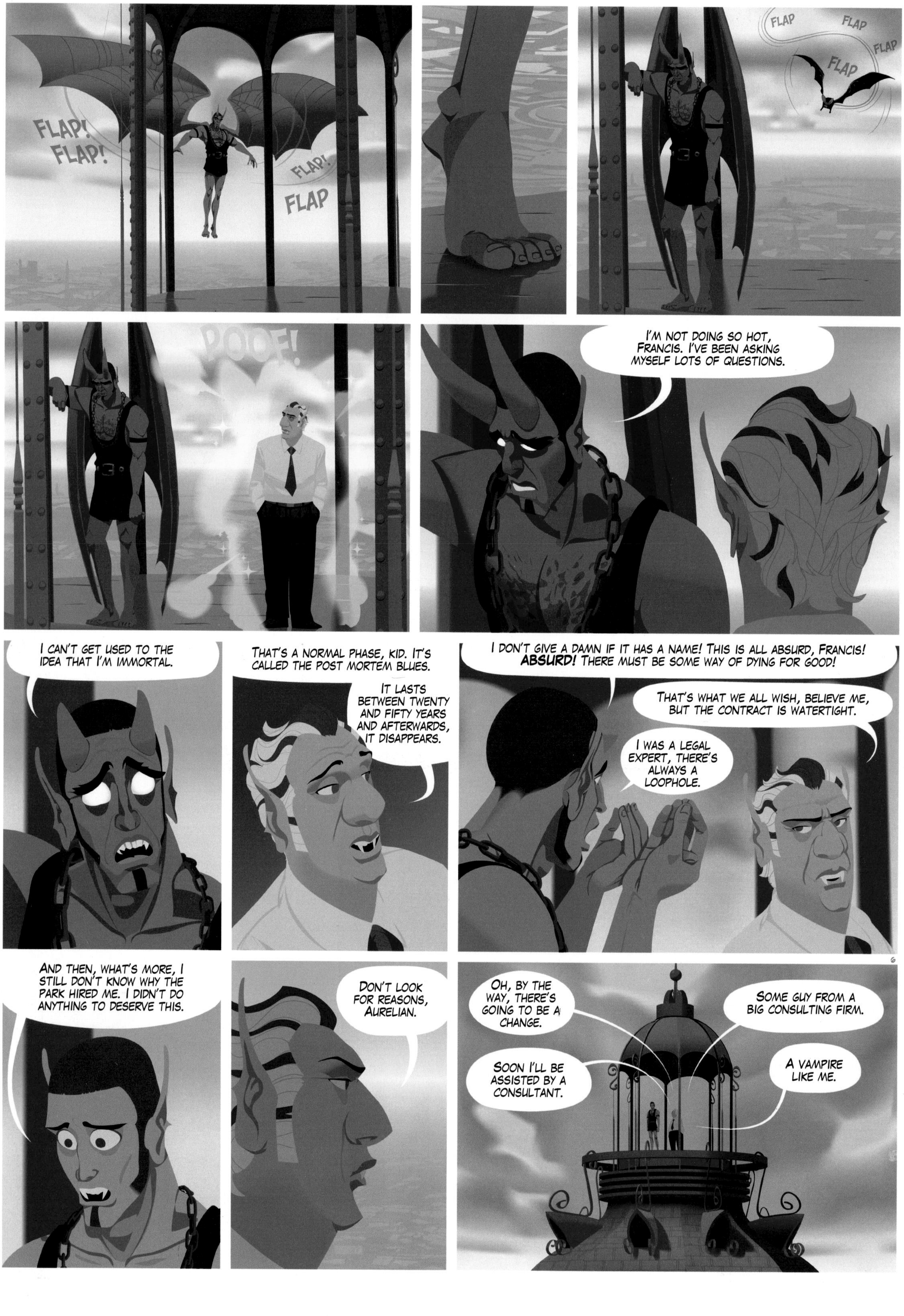
FLAP! FLAP!
FLAP! FLAP
FLAP FLAP FLAP FLAP
POOF!
I'M NOT DOING SO HOT, FRANCIS. I'VE BEEN ASKING MYSELF LOTS OF QUESTIONS.
I CAN'T GET USED TO THE IDEA THAT I'M IMMORTAL.
THAT'S A NORMAL PHASE, KID. IT'S CALLED THE POST MORTEM BLUES.
IT LASTS BETWEEN TWENTY AND FIFTY YEARS AND AFTERWARDS, IT DISAPPEARS.
I DON'T GIVE A DAMN IF IT HAS A NAME! THIS IS ALL ABSURD, FRANCIS! ABSURD! THERE MUST BE SOME WAY OF DYING FOR GOOD!
THAT'S WHAT WE ALL WISH, BELIEVE ME, BUT THE CONTRACT IS WATERTIGHT.
I WAS A LEGAL EXPERT, THERE'S ALWAYS A LOOPHOLE.
AND THEN, WHAT'S MORE, I STILL DON'T KNOW WHY THE PARK HIRED ME. I DIDN'T DO ANYTHING TO DESERVE THIS.
DON'T LOOK FOR REASONS, AURELIAN.
OH, BY THE WAY, THERE'S GOING TO BE A CHANGE.
SOME GUY FROM A BIG CONSULTING FIRM.
SOON I'LL BE ASSISTED BY A CONSULTANT.
A VAMPIRE LIKE ME.

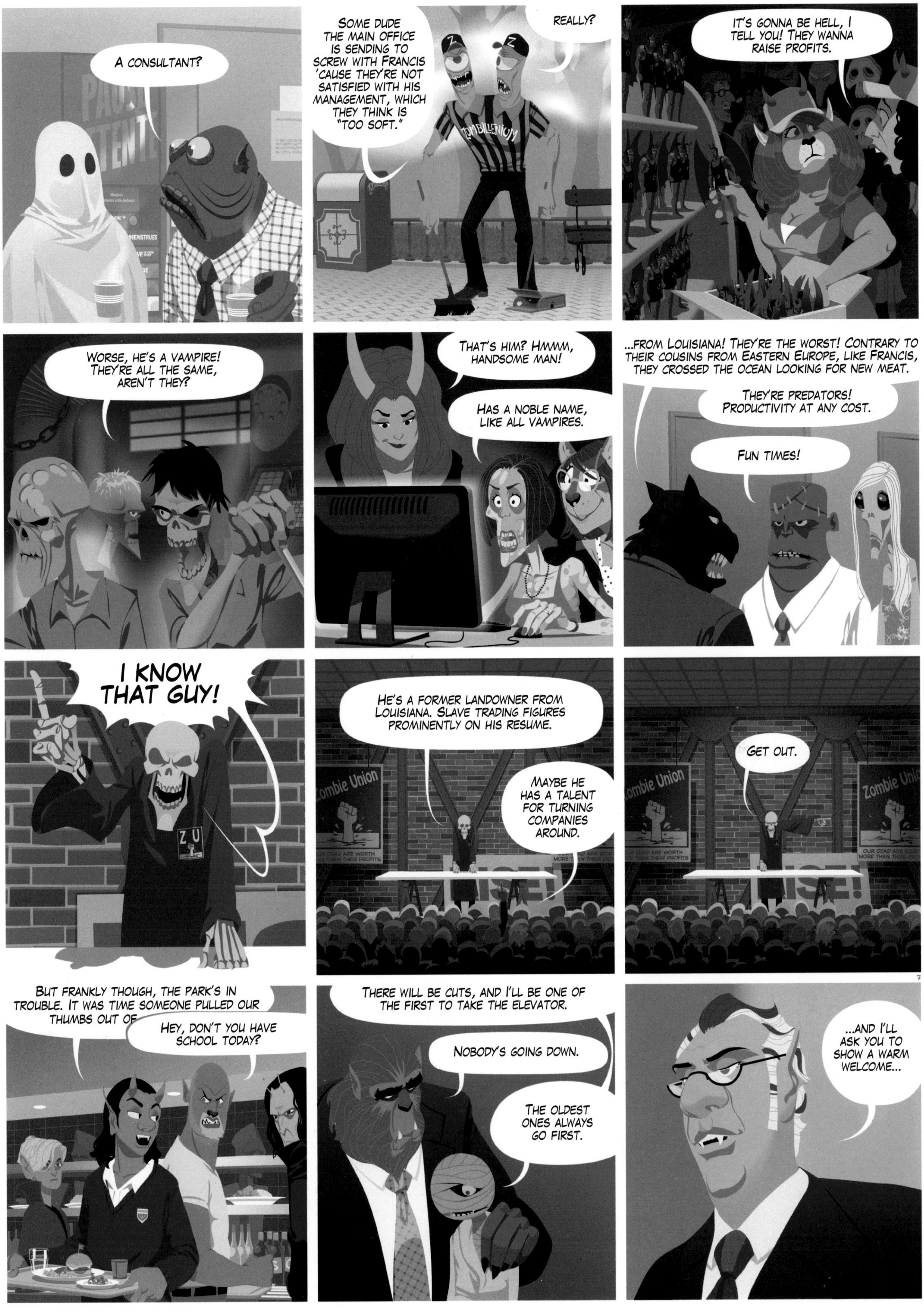
A CONSULTANT?
SOME DUDE THE MAIN OFFICE IS SENDING TO SCREW WITH FRANCIS 'CAUSE THEY'RE NOT SATISFIED WITH HIS MANAGEMENT, WHICH THEY THINK IS "TOO SOFT."
REALLY?
IT'S GONNA BE HELL, I TELL YOU! THEY WANNA RAISE PROFITS.
WORSE, HE'S A VAMPIRE! THEY'RE ALL THE SAME, AREN'T THEY?
THAT'S HIM? HMMM, HANDSOME MAN!
HAS A NOBLE NAME, LIKE ALL VAMPIRES.
...FROM LOUISIANA! THEY'RE THE WORST! CONTRARY TO THEIR COUSINS FROM EASTERN EUROPE, LIKE FRANCIS, THEY CROSSED THE OCEAN LOOKING FOR NEW MEAT.
THEY'RE PREDATORS! PRODUCTIVITY AT ANY COST.
FUN TIMES!
I KNOW THAT GUY!
ZU
HE'S A FORMER LANDOWNER FROM LOUISIANA. SLAVE TRADING FIGURES PROMINENTLY ON HIS RESUME.
MAYBE HE HAS A TALENT FOR TURNING COMPANIES AROUND.
Zombie Union
GET OUT.
Zombie Union
BUT FRANKLY THOUGH, THE PARK'S IN TROUBLE. IT WAS TIME SOMEONE PULLED OUR THUMBS OUT OF...
HEY, DON'T YOU HAVE SCHOOL TODAY?
THERE WILL BE CUTS, AND I'LL BE ONE OF THE FIRST TO TAKE THE ELEVATOR.
NOBODY'S GOING DOWN.
THE OLDEST ONES ALWAYS GO FIRST.
...AND I'LL ASK YOU TO SHOW A WARM WELCOME...

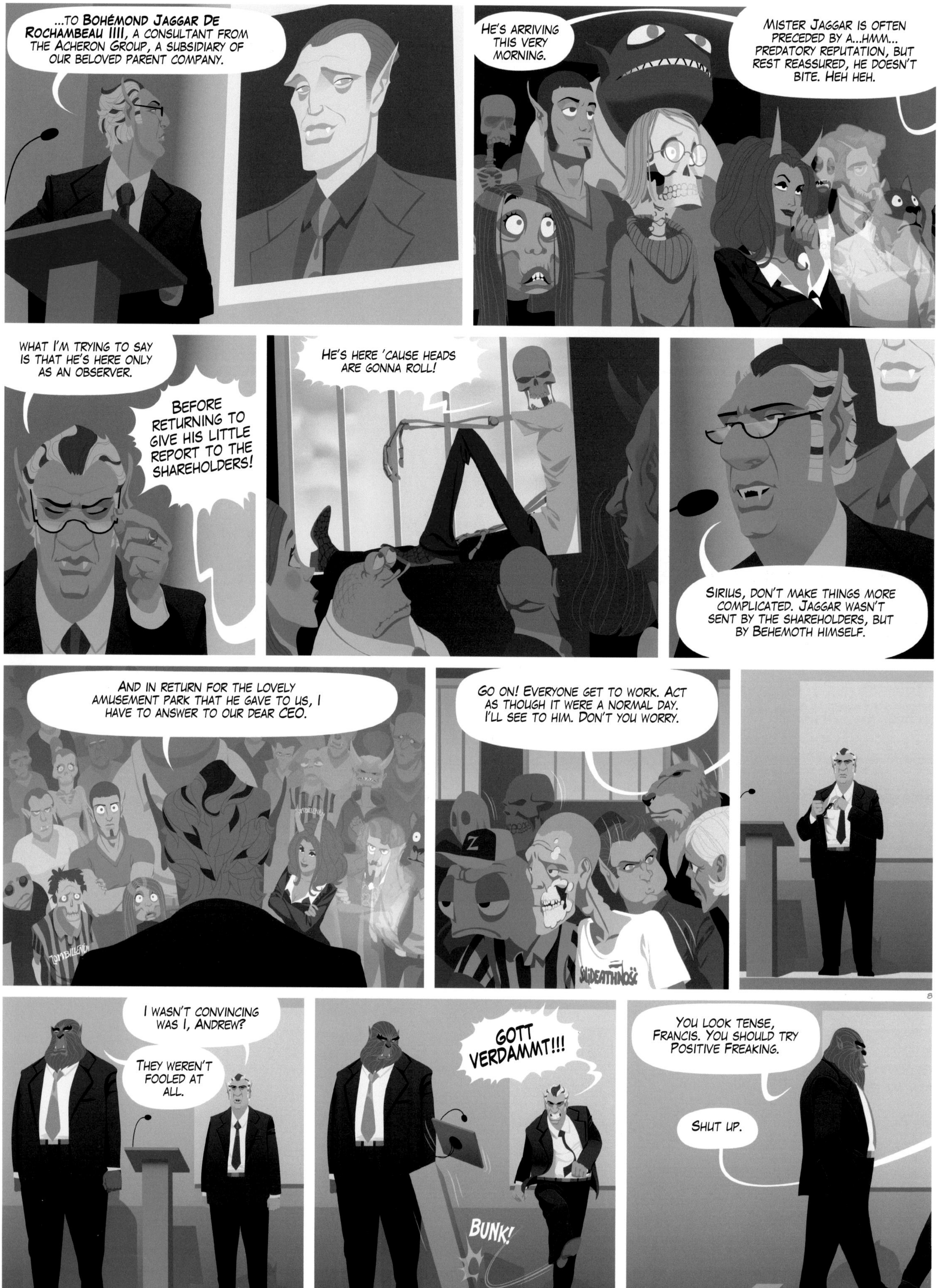

...TO BOHÉMOND JAGGAR DE ROCHAMBEAU IIII, A CONSULTANT FROM THE ACHERON GROUP, A SUBSIDIARY OF OUR BELOVED PARENT COMPANY.
HE'S ARRIVING THIS VERY MORNING.
MISTER JAGGAR IS OFTEN PRECEDED BY A...HMM... PREDATORY REPUTATION, BUT REST REASSURED, HE DOESN'T BITE. HEH HEH.
WHAT I'M TRYING TO SAY IS THAT HE'S HERE ONLY AS AN OBSERVER.
BEFORE RETURNING TO GIVE HIS LITTLE REPORT TO THE SHAREHOLDERS!
HE'S HERE 'CAUSE HEADS ARE GONNA ROLL!
SIRIUS, DON'T MAKE THINGS MORE COMPLICATED. JAGGAR WASN'T SENT BY THE SHAREHOLDERS, BUT BY BEHEMOTH HIMSELF.
AND IN RETURN FOR THE LOVELY AMUSEMENT PARK THAT HE GAVE TO US, I HAVE TO ANSWER TO OUR DEAR CEO.
GO ON! EVERYONE GET TO WORK. ACT AS THOUGH IT WERE A NORMAL DAY. I'LL SEE TO HIM. DON'T YOU WORRY.
I WASN'T CONVINCING WAS I, ANDREW?
THEY WEREN'T FOOLED AT ALL.
GOTT VERDAMMT!!!
BUNK!
YOU LOOK TENSE, FRANCIS. YOU SHOULD TRY POSITIVE FREAKING.
SHUT UP.

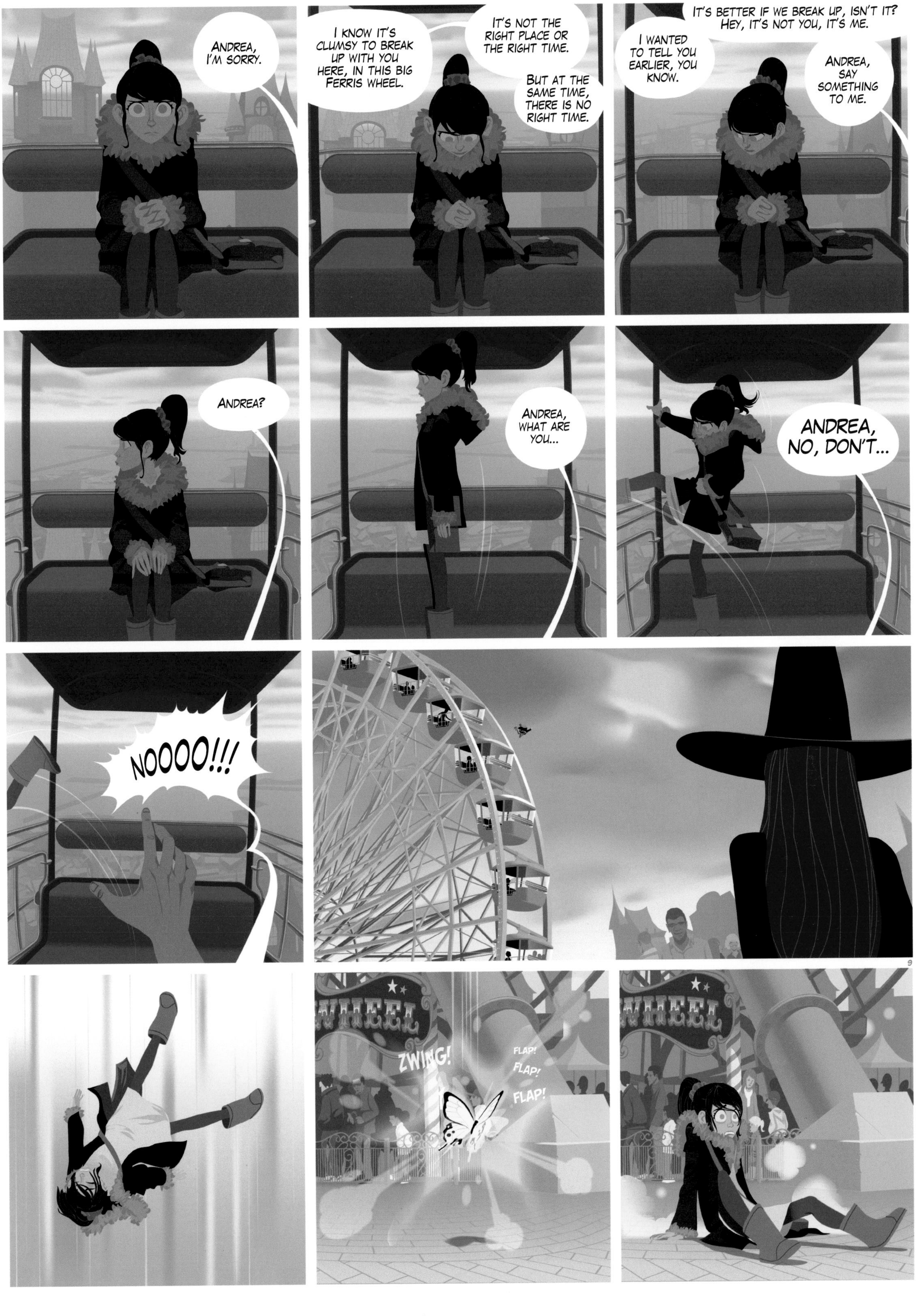

Andrea, I'm sorry.
I know it's clumsy to break up with you here, in this big Ferris wheel.
It's not the right place or the right time.
But at the same time, there is no right time.
It's better if we break up, isn't it? Hey, it's not you, it's me.
I wanted to tell you earlier, you know.
Andrea, say something to me.
Andrea?
Andrea, what are you...
ANDREA, NO, DON'T...
NOOOO!!!
WHEEL
ZWING!
FLAP!
FLAP!
FLAP!
WHEEL

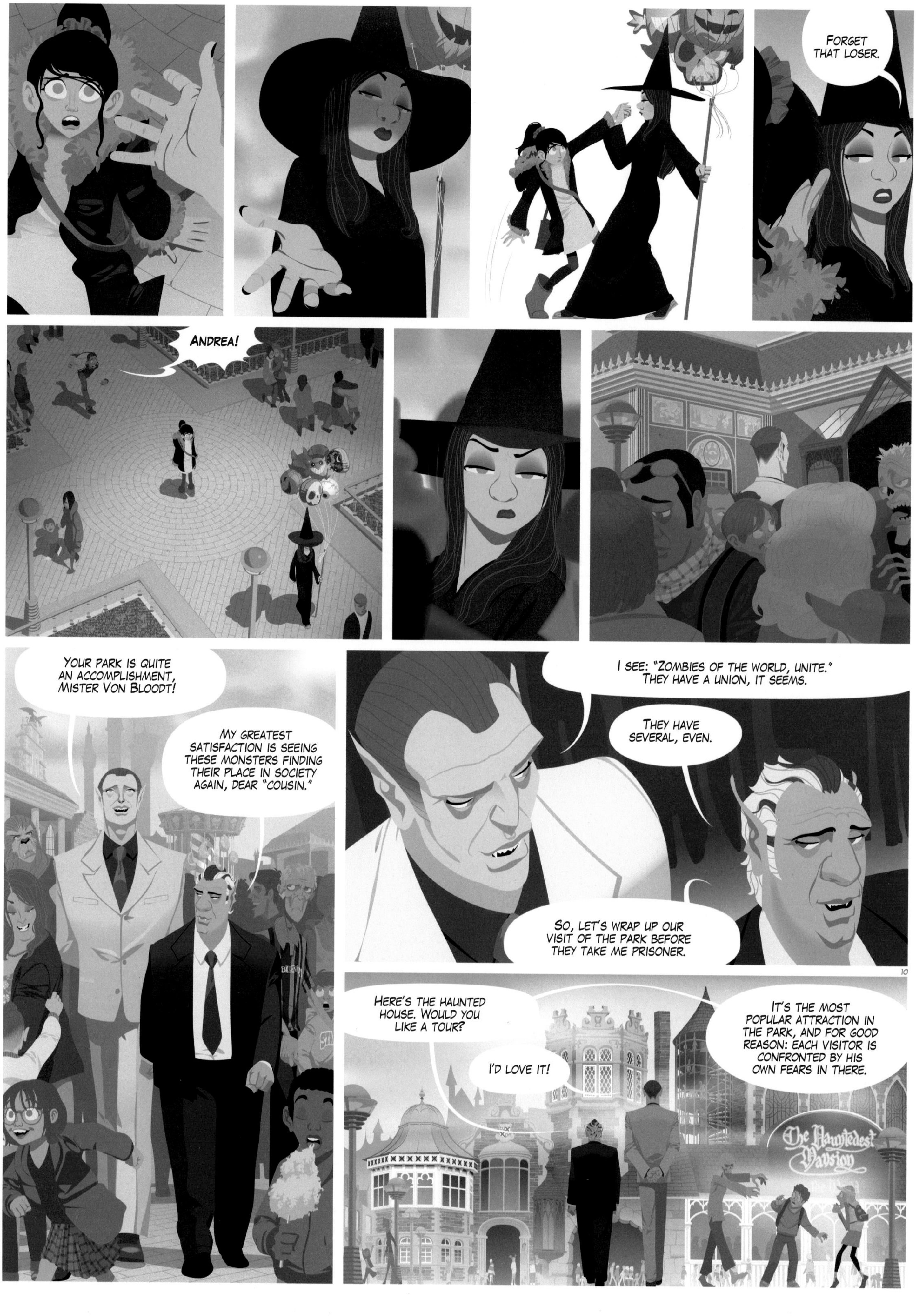
Forget that loser.
Andrea!
Your park is quite an accomplishment, Mister Von Bloodt!
My greatest satisfaction is seeing these monsters finding their place in society again, dear "cousin."
I see: "Zombies of the world, unite." They have a union, it seems.
They have several, even.
So, let's wrap up our visit of the park before they take me prisoner.
Here's the haunted house. Would you like a tour?
I'd love it!
It's the most popular attraction in the park, and for good reason: each visitor is confronted by his own fears in there.
The Hauntedest Mansion

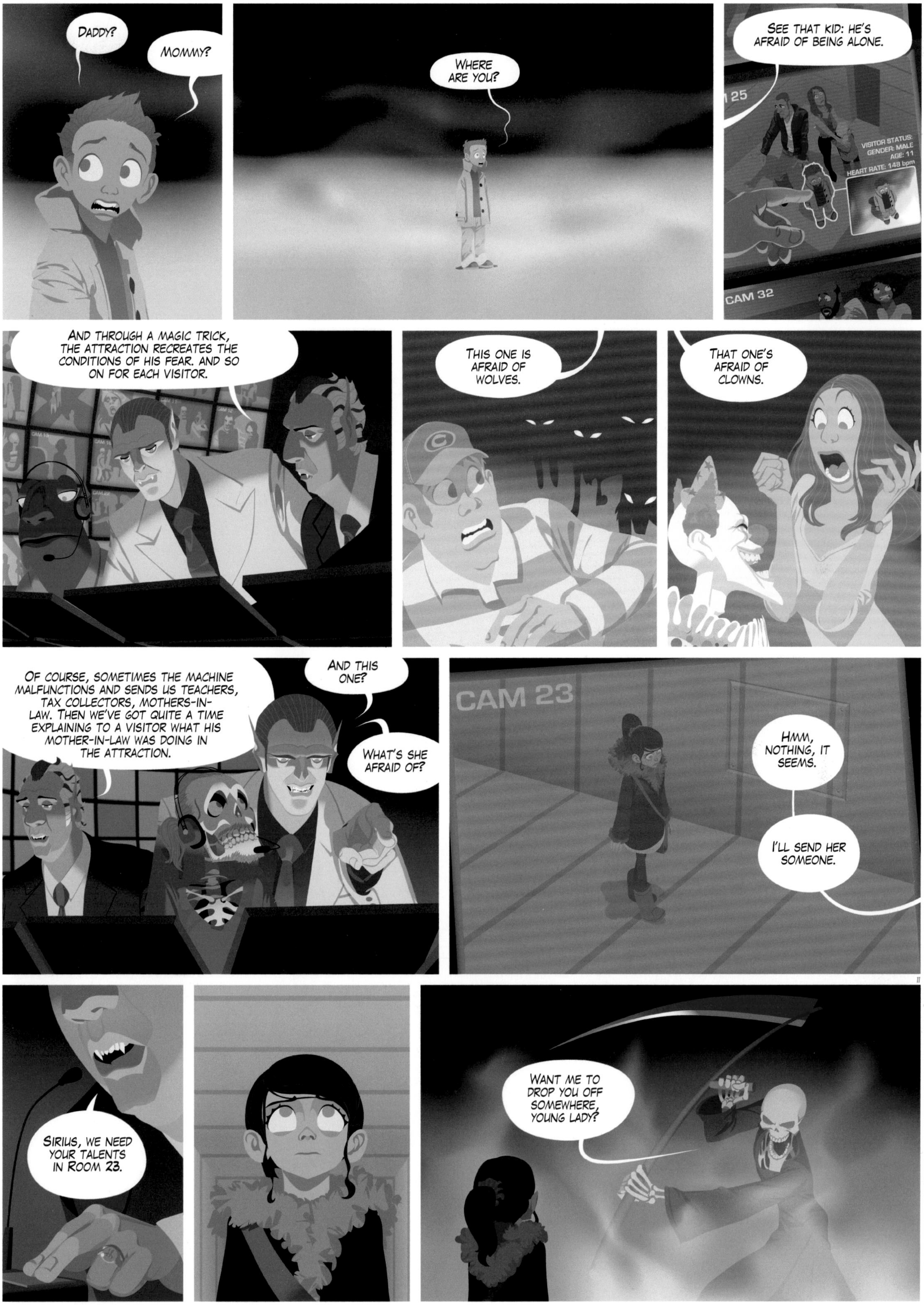

DADDY?
MOMMY?
WHERE ARE YOU?
SEE THAT KID: HE'S AFRAID OF BEING ALONE.
CAM 25
VISITOR STATUS:
GENDER: MALE
AGE: 11
HEART RATE: 148 bpm
CAM 32
AND THROUGH A MAGIC TRICK, THE ATTRACTION RECREATES THE CONDITIONS OF HIS FEAR. AND SO ON FOR EACH VISITOR.
THIS ONE IS AFRAID OF WOLVES.
THAT ONE'S AFRAID OF CLOWNS.
OF COURSE, SOMETIMES THE MACHINE MALFUNCTIONS AND SENDS US TEACHERS, TAX COLLECTORS, MOTHERS-IN-LAW. THEN WE'VE GOT QUITE A TIME EXPLAINING TO A VISITOR WHAT HIS MOTHER-IN-LAW WAS DOING IN THE ATTRACTION.
AND THIS ONE?
WHAT'S SHE AFRAID OF?
CAM 23
HMM, NOTHING, IT SEEMS.
I'LL SEND HER SOMEONE.
SIRIUS, WE NEED YOUR TALENTS IN ROOM 23.
WANT ME TO DROP YOU OFF SOMEWHERE, YOUNG LADY?

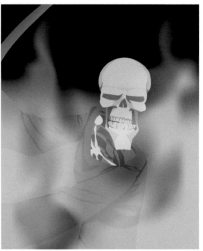

FRANCIS! WHAT DO I DO?

AHH, FORGET IT.

AND WHILE YOU'RE AT IT, FRESHEN UP YOUR LINES.

THAT YOUNG PERSON ISN'T AFRAID BECAUSE SHE NO LONGER CARES ABOUT LIFE.

I'VE ALWAYS BEEN INTRIGUED BY HUMANS WHO AREN'T AFRAID.

WITH YOUR PERMISSION, MY DEAR FRANCIS, I'D LIKE TO GIVE IT A TRY.

TO SCARE HER? WHY NOT? IF THAT AMUSES YOU.

"GO ON, I'LL TEACH YOU YOUR JOB, WITHOUT EVER HAVING SET FOOT IN AN AMUSEMENT PARK."

OKAY, JOSEPH, WHERE CAN WE FOLLOW HIM?

ON THIS SCREEN, BOSS!

YES, GRETCHEN?

A YOUNG LADY WITH A PONYTAIL?

TEE DEE DEE TEE DEE DEE TEE

CAM 33

WITH A PARKA WITH A FLUFFLY HOOD?

I'M LOOKING RIGHT AT HER, YES.

12

HUH?

WATCH OUT FOR HER?

WAIT, HANG ON.

WHOAWHOAWHOA! HE'S TOUCHING HER! THAT'S AGAINST THE RULES!

GOTT VERDAMMT!

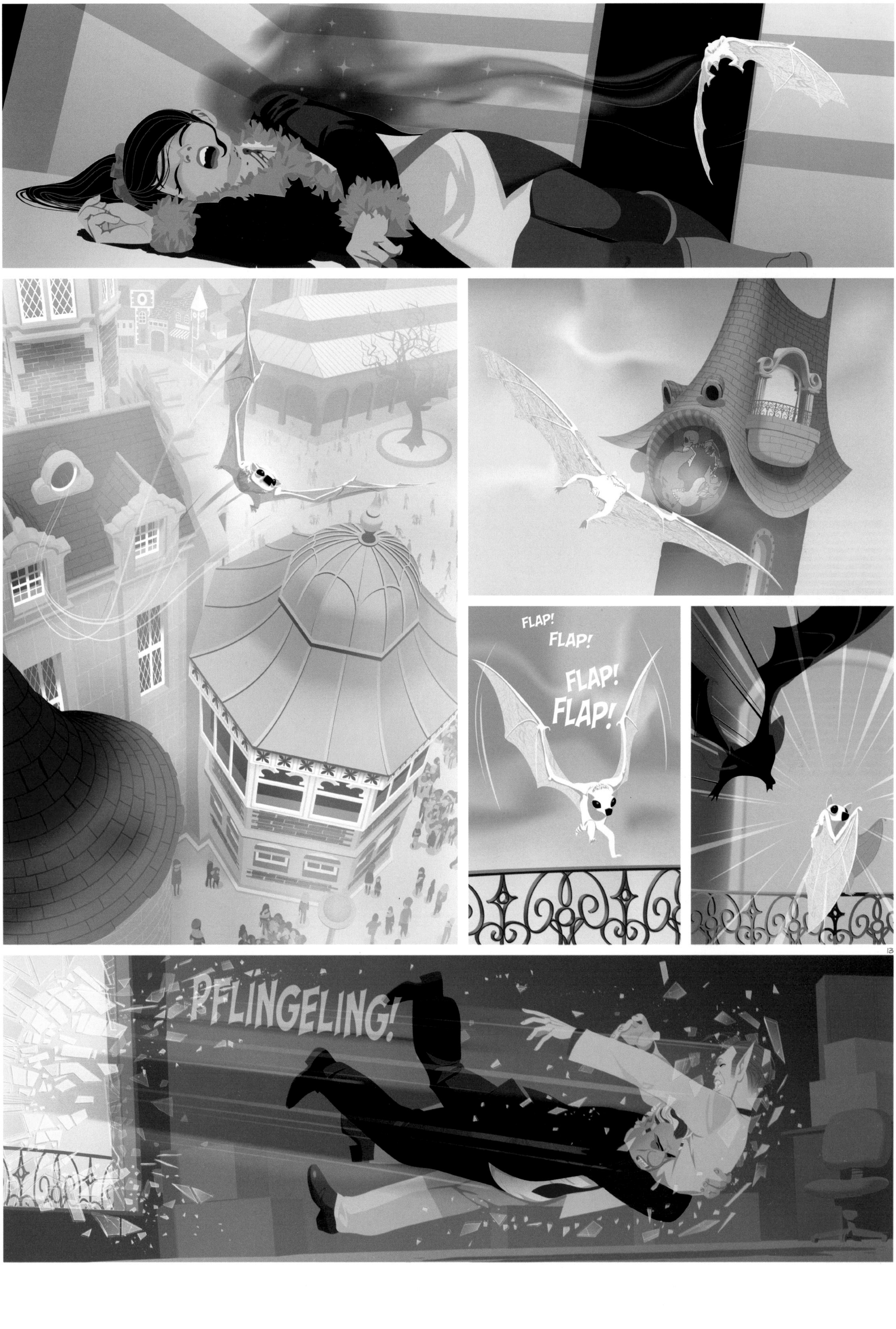
FLAP!
FLAP!
FLAP!
FLAP!
PFLINGELING!

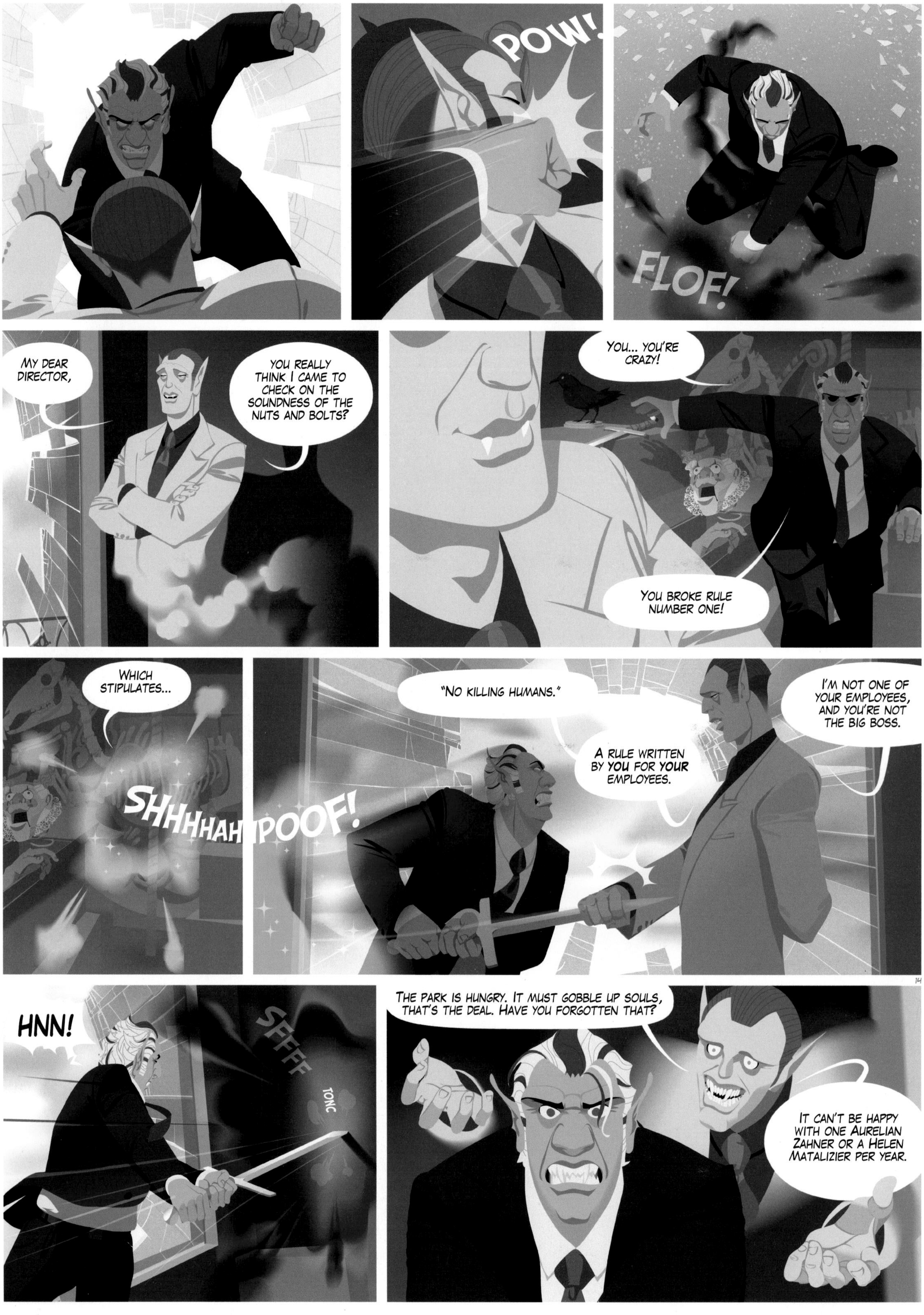
POW!
FLOF!
My dear director,
You really think I came to check on the soundness of the nuts and bolts?
You... you're crazy!
You broke rule number one!
Which stipulates...
SHHHHAH
POOF!
"No killing humans."
A rule written by **you** for **your** employees.
I'm not one of your employees, and you're not the big boss.
HNN!
SFFFF
TONC
The park is hungry. It must gobble up souls, that's the deal. Have you forgotten that?
It can't be happy with one Aurelian Zahner or a Helen Matalizier per year.

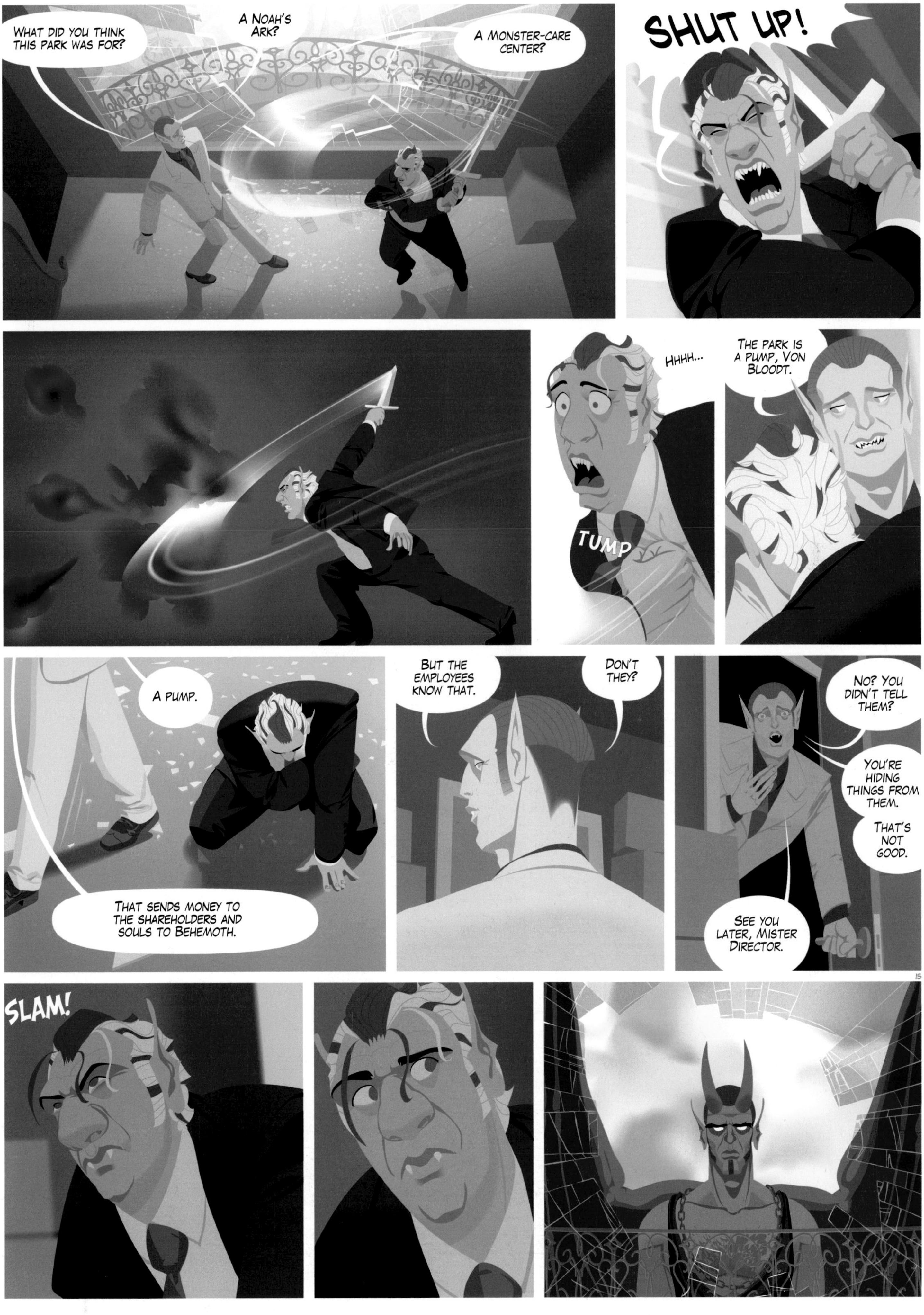

What did you think this park was for?
A Noah's Ark?
A Monster-care center?
SHUT UP!
HHHH...
TUMP
The park is a pump, Von Bloodt.
A pump.
That sends money to the shareholders and souls to Behemoth.
But the employees know that.
Don't they?
No? You didn't tell them?
You're hiding things from them.
That's not good.
See you later, Mister Director.
SLAM!

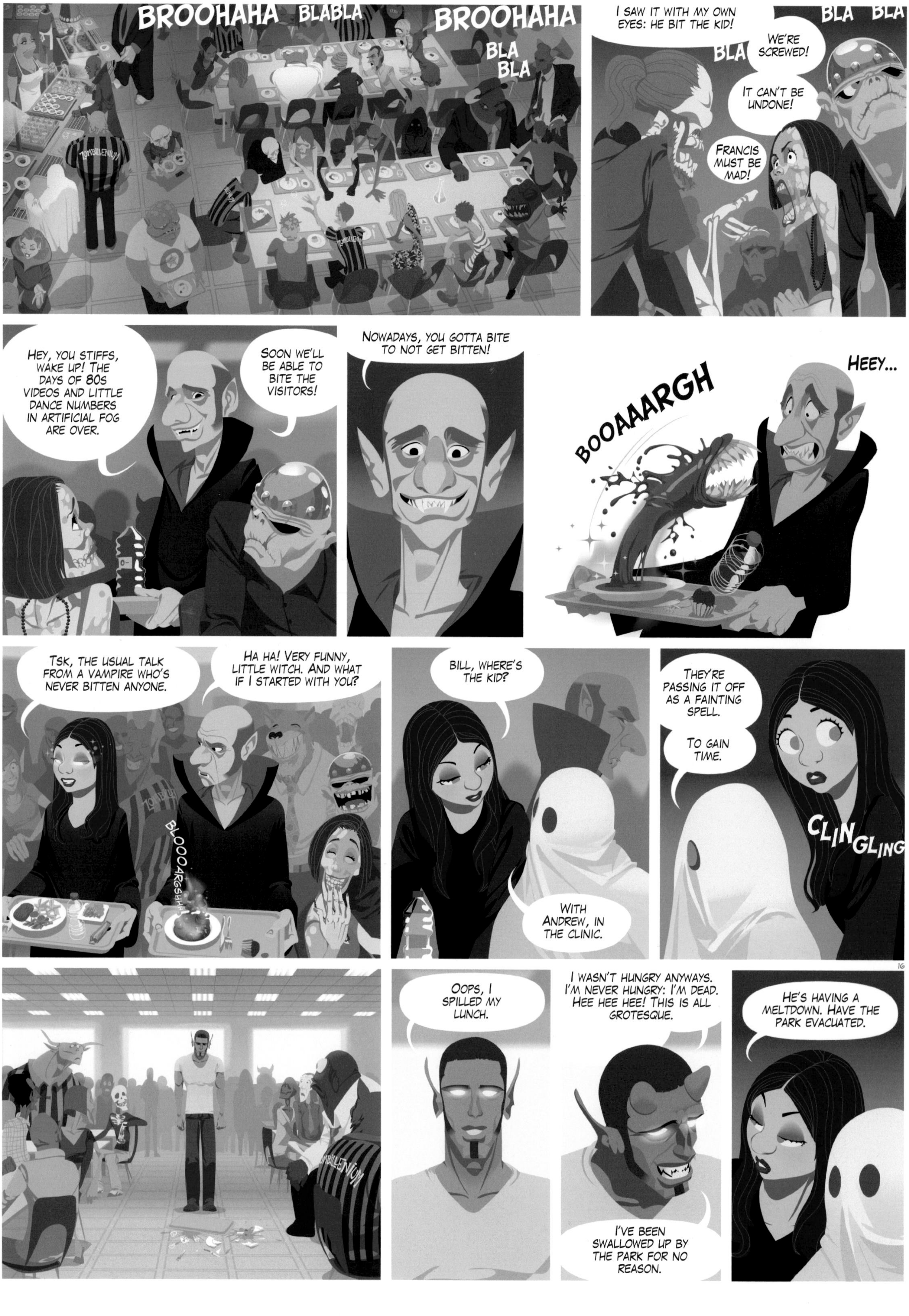
BROOHAHA
BLABLA
BROOHAHA
BLA BLA
ZOMBILLENIUM
I SAW IT WITH MY OWN EYES: HE BIT THE KID!
BLA
BLA BLA
WE'RE SCREWED!
IT CAN'T BE UNDONE!
FRANCIS MUST BE MAD!
HEY, YOU STIFFS, WAKE UP! THE DAYS OF 80s VIDEOS AND LITTLE DANCE NUMBERS IN ARTIFICIAL FOG ARE OVER.
SOON WE'LL BE ABLE TO BITE THE VISITORS!
NOWADAYS, YOU GOTTA BITE TO NOT GET BITTEN!
HEEY...
BOOAAARGH
TSK, THE USUAL TALK FROM A VAMPIRE WHO'S NEVER BITTEN ANYONE.
HA HA! VERY FUNNY, LITTLE WITCH. AND WHAT IF I STARTED WITH YOU?
BLOOOARGSHH
BILL, WHERE'S THE KID?
WITH ANDREW, IN THE CLINIC.
THEY'RE PASSING IT OFF AS A FAINTING SPELL.
TO GAIN TIME.
CLINGLING
OOPS, I SPILLED MY LUNCH.
I WASN'T HUNGRY ANYWAYS. I'M NEVER HUNGRY: I'M DEAD. HEE HEE HEE! THIS IS ALL GROTESQUE.
I'VE BEEN SWALLOWED UP BY THE PARK FOR NO REASON.
HE'S HAVING A MELTDOWN. HAVE THE PARK EVACUATED.

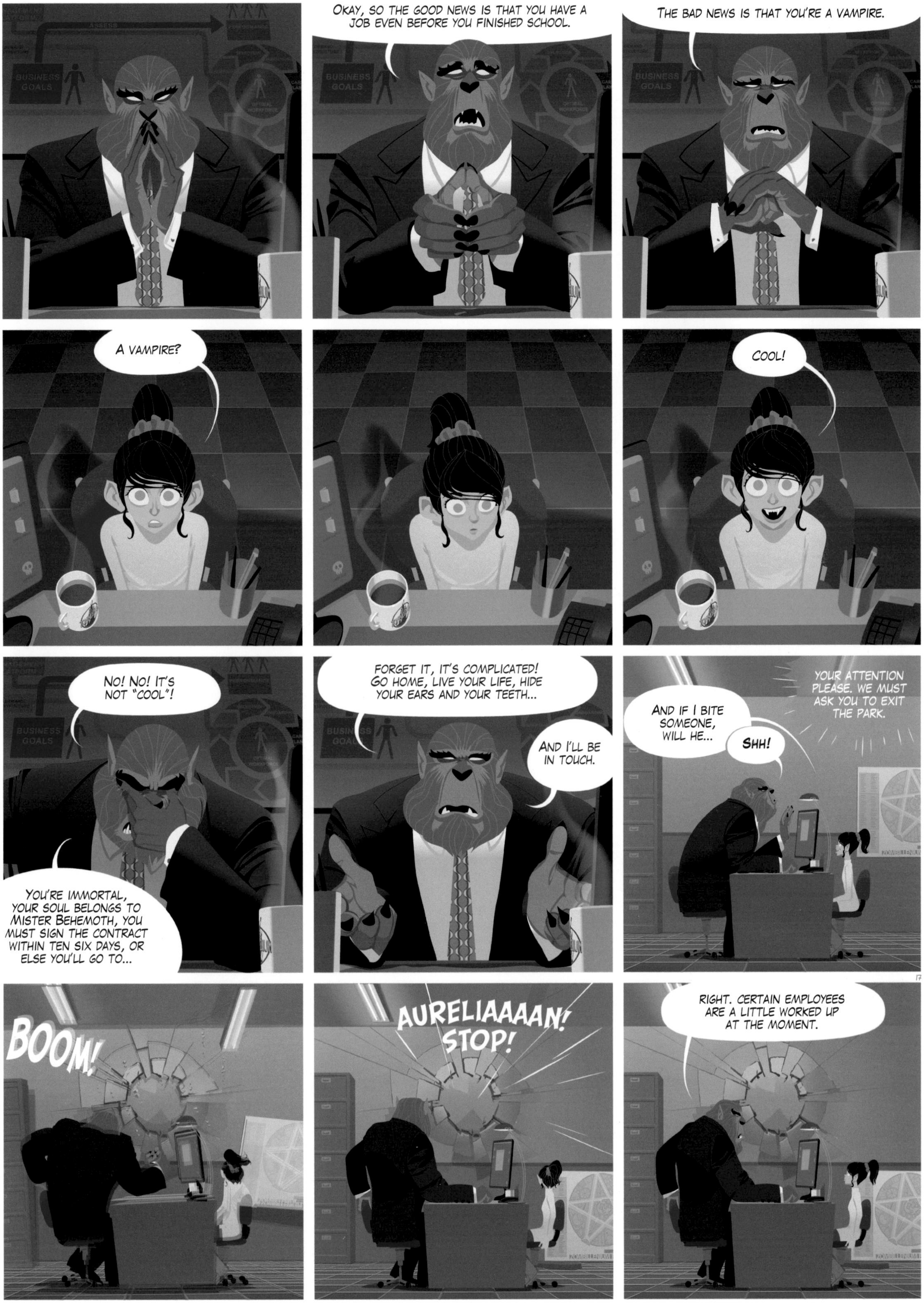

Okay, so the good news is that you have a job even before you finished school.
The bad news is that you're a vampire.
A vampire?
Cool!
No! No! It's not "cool"!
You're immortal, your soul belongs to Mister Behemoth, you must sign the contract within ten six days, or else you'll go to...
Forget it, it's complicated! Go home, live your life, hide your ears and your teeth...
And I'll be in touch.
And if I bite someone, will he...
Shh!
Your attention please. We must ask you to exit the park.
BOOM!
AURELIAAAAN! STOP!
Right. Certain employees are a little worked up at the moment.

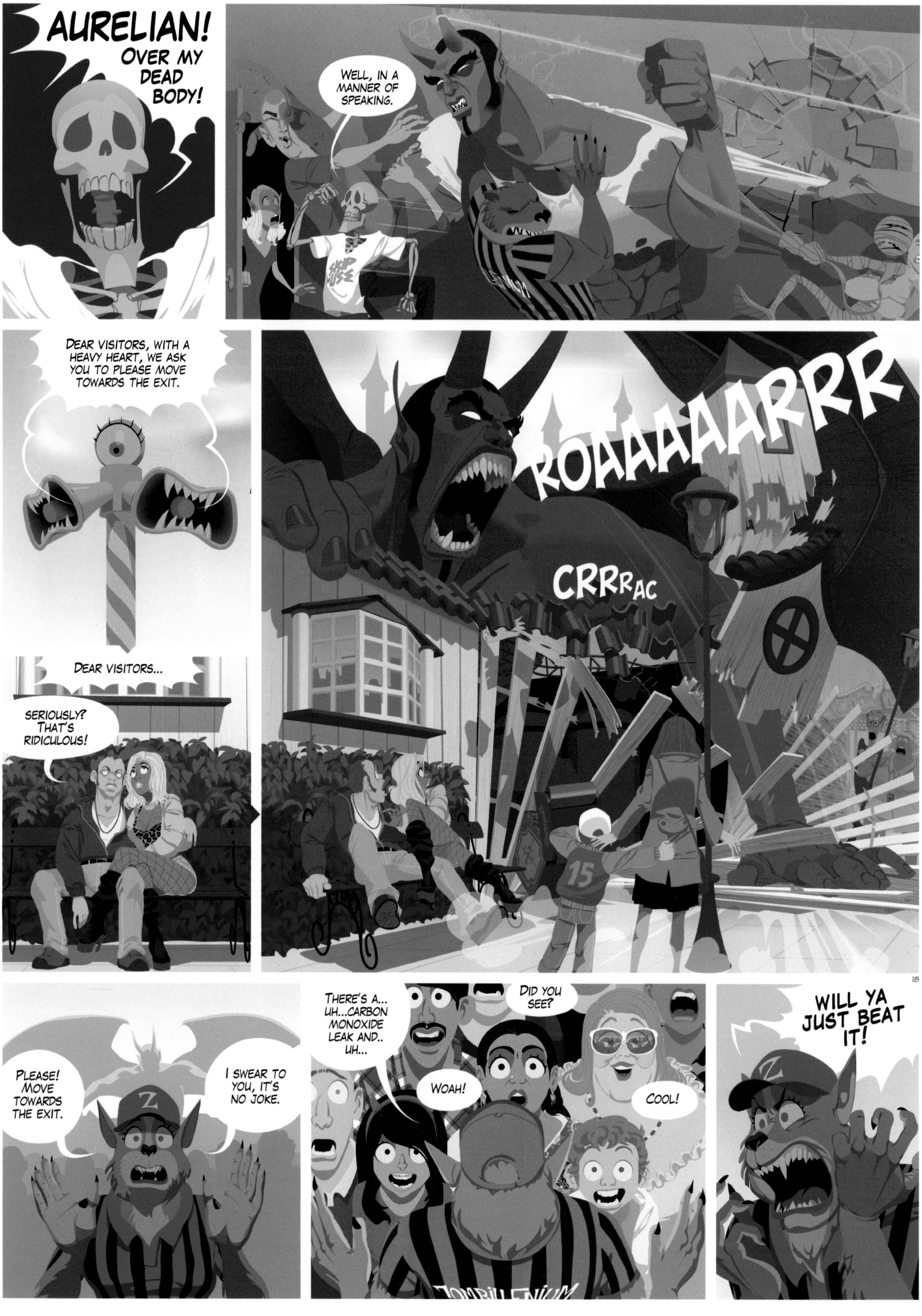
AURELIAN! OVER MY DEAD BODY!
WELL, IN A MANNER OF SPEAKING.
DEAR VISITORS, WITH A HEAVY HEART, WE ASK YOU TO PLEASE MOVE TOWARDS THE EXIT.
DEAR VISITORS...
SERIOUSLY? THAT'S RIDICULOUS!
ROAAAAARRR
CRRRAC
PLEASE! MOVE TOWARDS THE EXIT.
I SWEAR TO YOU, IT'S NO JOKE.
THERE'S A... UH...CARBON MONOXIDE LEAK AND.. UH...
DID YOU SEE?
WOAH!
COOL!
WILL YA JUST BEAT IT!

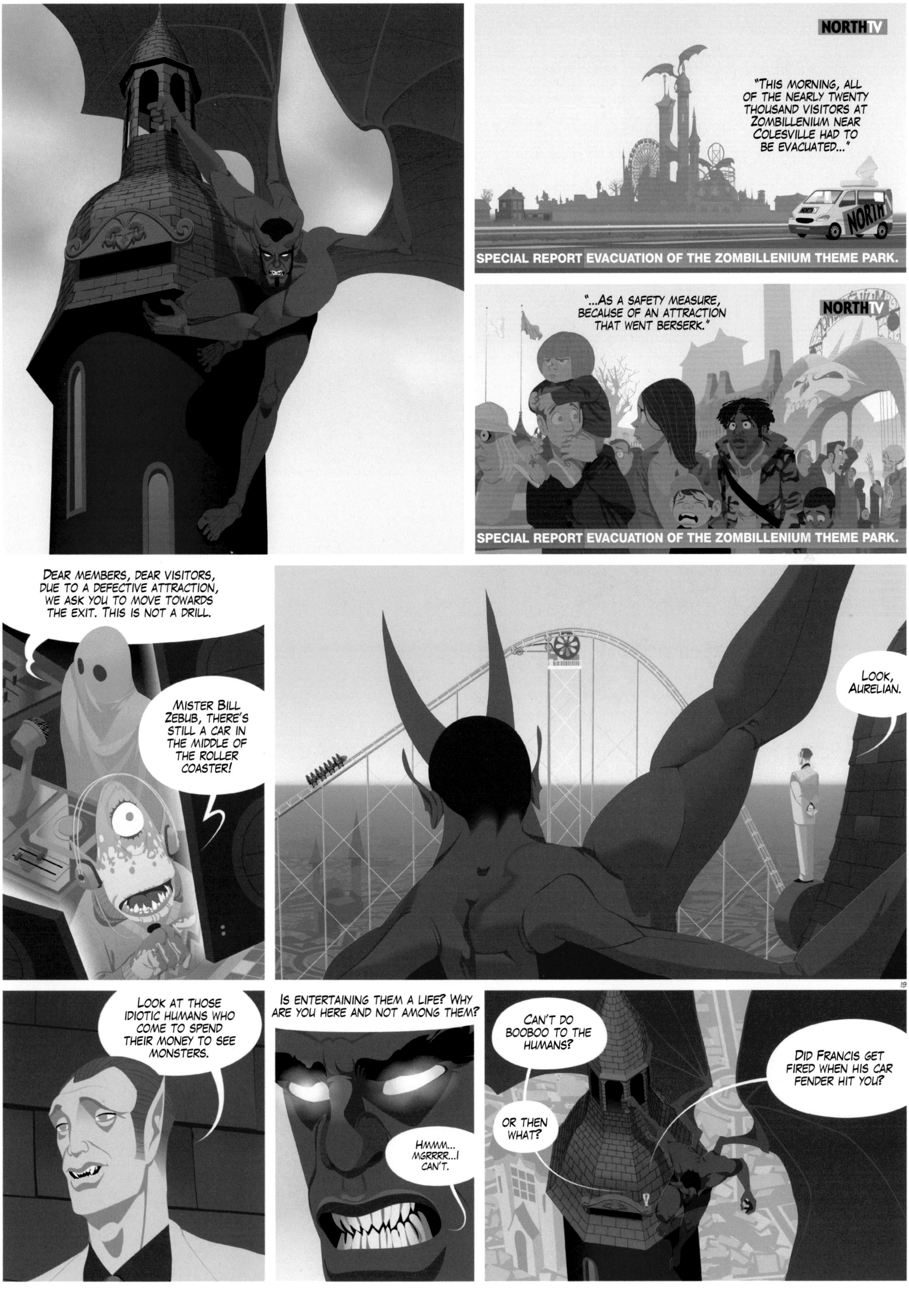

NORTH TV
"This morning, all of the nearly twenty thousand visitors at Zombillenium near Colesville had to be evacuated..."
SPECIAL REPORT EVACUATION OF THE ZOMBILLENIUM THEME PARK.
"...As a safety measure, because of an attraction that went berserk."
NORTH TV
SPECIAL REPORT EVACUATION OF THE ZOMBILLENIUM THEME PARK.
Dear members, dear visitors, due to a defective attraction, we ask you to move towards the exit. This is not a drill.
Mister Bill Zebub, there's still a car in the middle of the roller coaster!
Look, Aurelian.
Look at those idiotic humans who come to spend their money to see monsters.
Is entertaining them a life? Why are you here and not among them?
Hmmm... mgrrrr...I can't.
Can't do booboo to the humans?
Or then what?
Did Francis get fired when his car fender hit you?

I HOPE OURS ISN'T THE DEFECTIVE ATTRACTION.

HEY! MISTER DEMON! COME HELP US!

HA HA HA!

WHERE'S HE GOING?

HE'S DOWN BELOW.

HE'S HEADING TOWARDS THE END OF THE DESCEN...

...T. WHAT?!

CRRRASH!

BAP!

EMERGENCY STOP

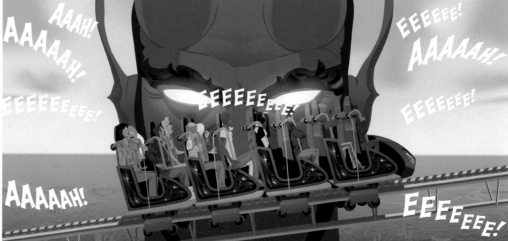

CLANG!

AAAH!

AAAAAH!

EEEEEEEEE!

EEEEEEEEEEE!

EEEEEEE!

AAAAAAH!

EEEEEEE!

AAAAAH!

EEEEEEEE!

WHEN I WAS A KID...

I HAD AN ELECTRIC TRAIN.

AND I LOVED TO CREATE ACCIDENTS.

AAAAAAH!

EEEEEEE!

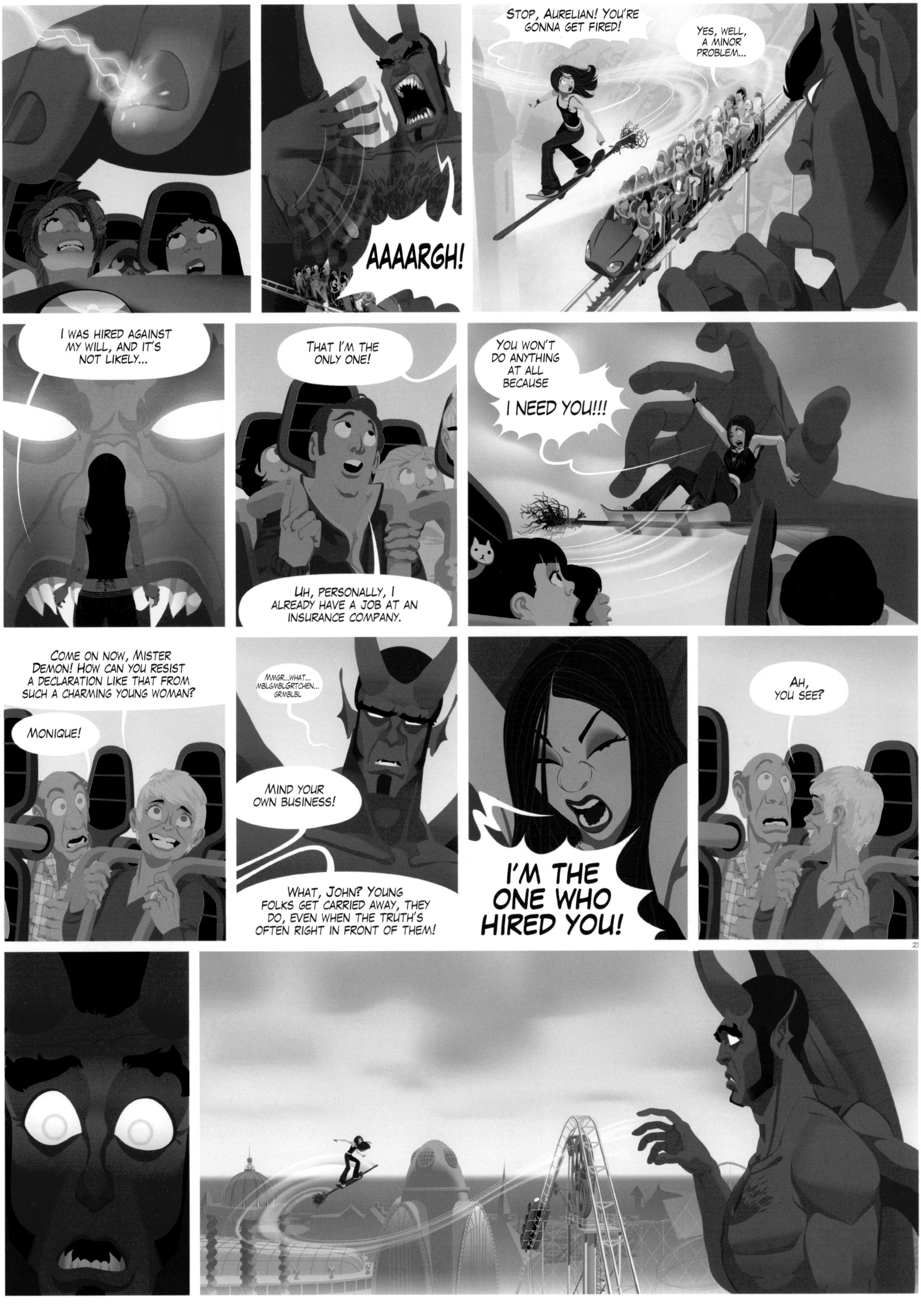
AAAARGH!
STOP, AURELIAN! YOU'RE GONNA GET FIRED!
YES, WELL, A MINOR PROBLEM...
I WAS HIRED AGAINST MY WILL, AND IT'S NOT LIKELY...
THAT I'M THE ONLY ONE!
UH, PERSONALLY, I ALREADY HAVE A JOB AT AN INSURANCE COMPANY.
YOU WON'T DO ANYTHING AT ALL BECAUSE
I NEED YOU!!!
COME ON NOW, MISTER DEMON! HOW CAN YOU RESIST A DECLARATION LIKE THAT FROM SUCH A CHARMING YOUNG WOMAN?
MONIQUE!
MMGR...WHAT... MBLGMBLGRTCHEN... GRMBLBL
MIND YOUR OWN BUSINESS!
WHAT, JOHN? YOUNG FOLKS GET CARRIED AWAY, THEY DO, EVEN WHEN THE TRUTH'S OFTEN RIGHT IN FRONT OF THEM!
I'M THE ONE WHO HIRED YOU!
AH, YOU SEE?

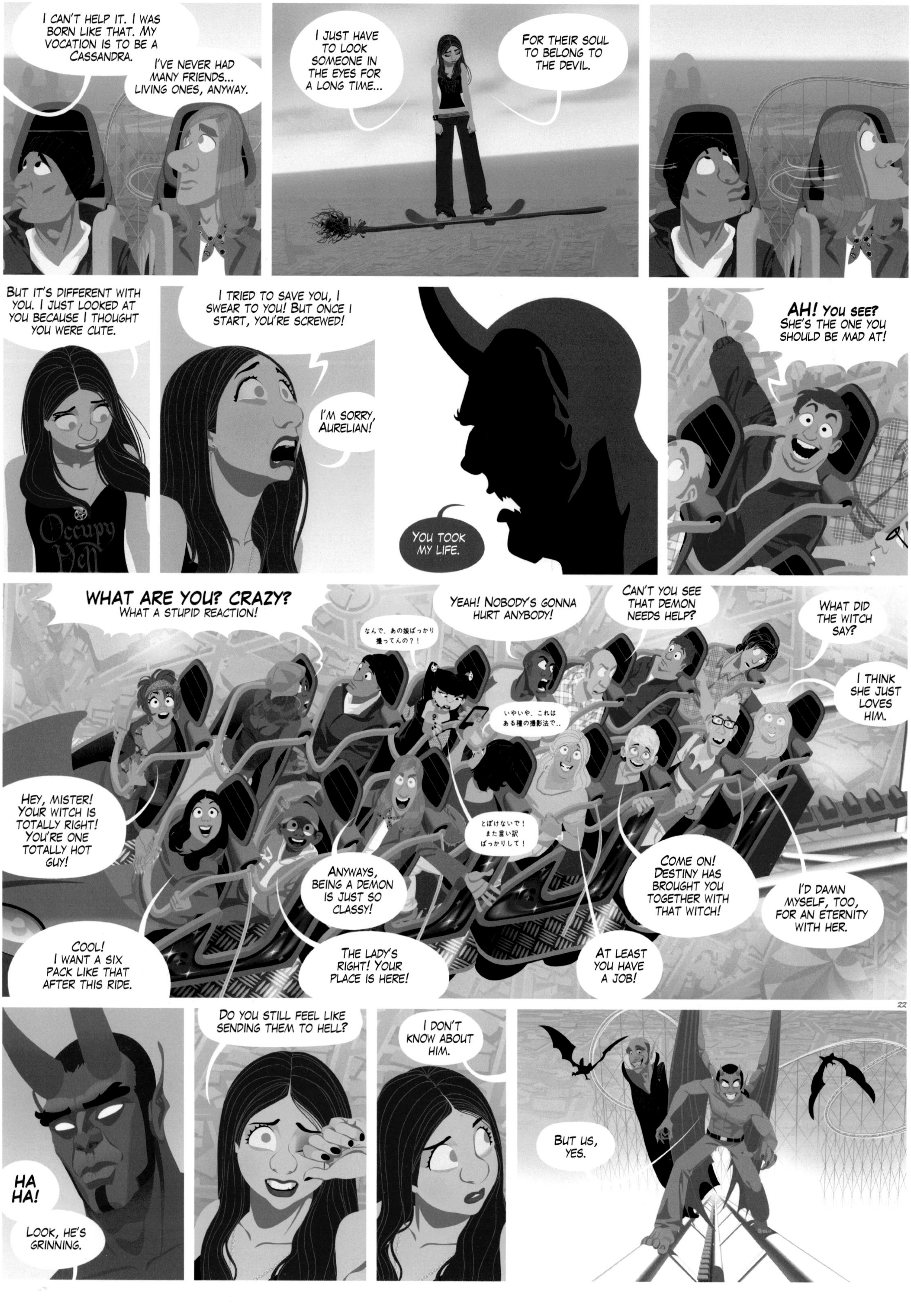
I CAN'T HELP IT. I WAS BORN LIKE THAT. MY VOCATION IS TO BE A CASSANDRA.
I'VE NEVER HAD MANY FRIENDS... LIVING ONES, ANYWAY.
I JUST HAVE TO LOOK SOMEONE IN THE EYES FOR A LONG TIME...
FOR THEIR SOUL TO BELONG TO THE DEVIL.
BUT IT'S DIFFERENT WITH YOU. I JUST LOOKED AT YOU BECAUSE I THOUGHT YOU WERE CUTE.
I TRIED TO SAVE YOU, I SWEAR TO YOU! BUT ONCE I START, YOU'RE SCREWED!
I'M SORRY, AURELIAN!
YOU TOOK MY LIFE.
AH! YOU SEE? SHE'S THE ONE YOU SHOULD BE MAD AT!
WHAT ARE YOU? CRAZY? WHAT A STUPID REACTION!
なんで、あの娘ばっかり撮ってんの？！
YEAH! NOBODY'S GONNA HURT ANYBODY!
CAN'T YOU SEE THAT DEMON NEEDS HELP?
WHAT DID THE WITCH SAY?
I THINK SHE JUST LOVES HIM.
いやいや、これはある種の撮影法で..
HEY, MISTER! YOUR WITCH IS TOTALLY RIGHT! YOU'RE ONE TOTALLY HOT GUY!
とぼけないで！また言い訳ばっかりして！
ANYWAYS, BEING A DEMON IS JUST SO CLASSY!
COME ON! DESTINY HAS BROUGHT YOU TOGETHER WITH THAT WITCH!
I'D DAMN MYSELF, TOO, FOR AN ETERNITY WITH HER.
COOL! I WANT A SIX PACK LIKE THAT AFTER THIS RIDE.
THE LADY'S RIGHT! YOUR PLACE IS HERE!
AT LEAST YOU HAVE A JOB!
HA HA!
LOOK, HE'S GRINNING.
DO YOU STILL FEEL LIKE SENDING THEM TO HELL?
I DON'T KNOW ABOUT HIM.
BUT US, YES.

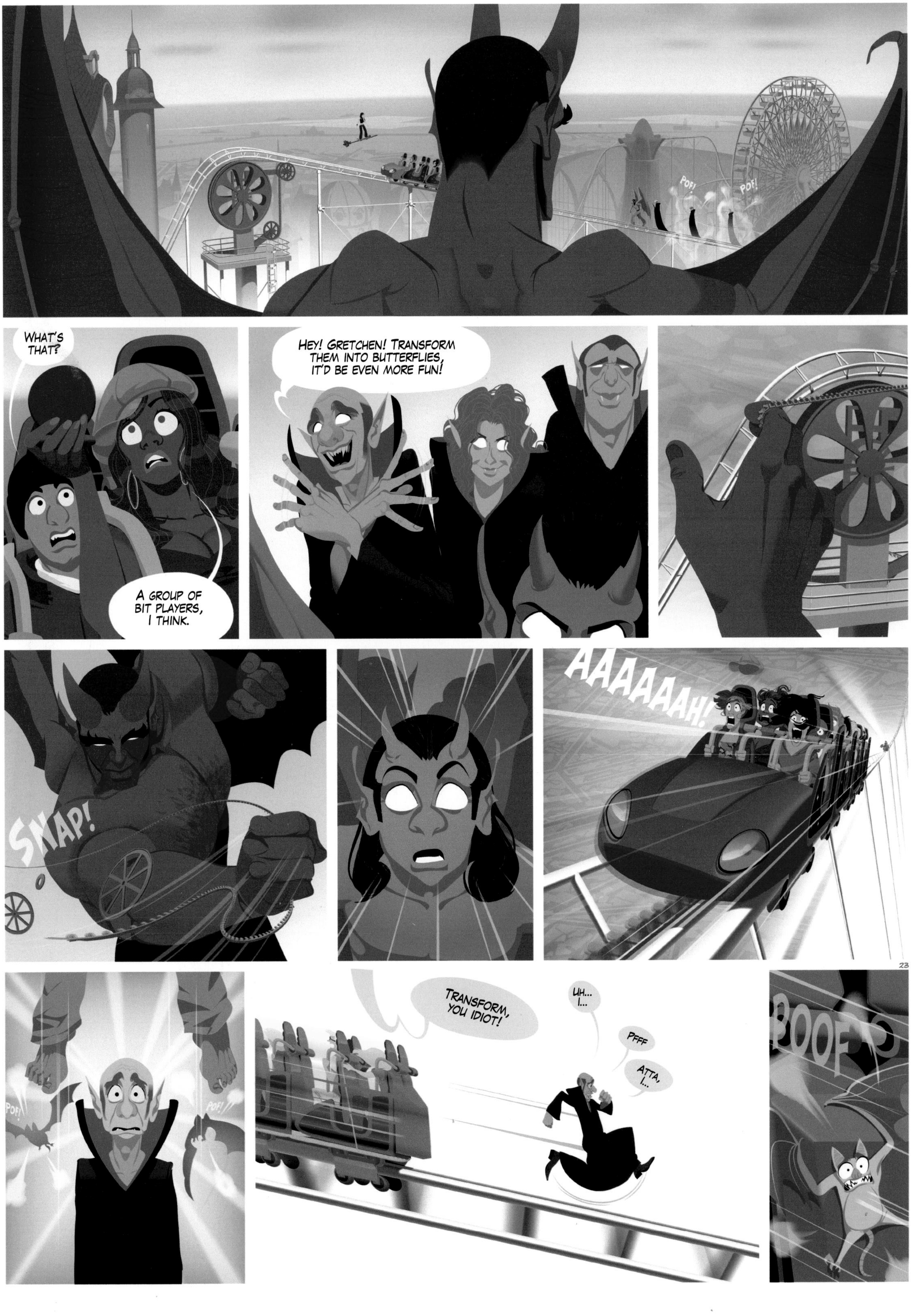
POF!
POF!
WHAT'S THAT?
A GROUP OF BIT PLAYERS, I THINK.
HEY! GRETCHEN! TRANSFORM THEM INTO BUTTERFLIES, IT'D BE EVEN MORE FUN!
SNAP!
AAAAAAH!
POF!
POF!
TRANSFORM, YOU IDIOT!
UH... I...
PFFF
ATTA, I...
POOF

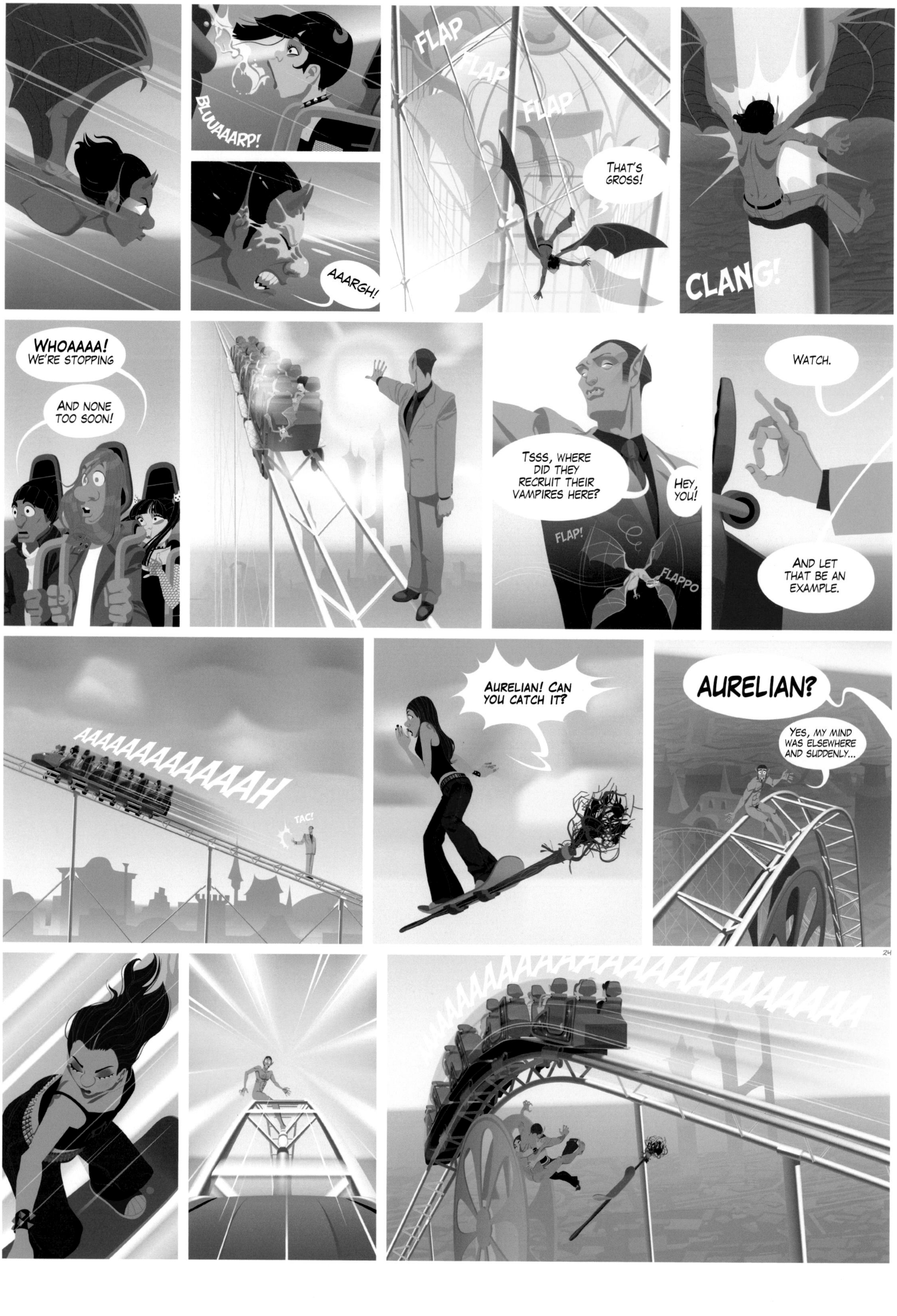
BLUUAAARP!
AAARGH!
FLAP
FLAP
FLAP
THAT'S GROSS!
CLANG!
WHOAAAA! WE'RE STOPPING
AND NONE TOO SOON!
TSSS, WHERE DID THEY RECRUIT THEIR VAMPIRES HERE?
HEY, YOU!
FLAP!
FLAPPO
WATCH.
AND LET THAT BE AN EXAMPLE.
AAAAAAAAAAAAAH
TAC!
AURELIAN! CAN YOU CATCH IT?
AURELIAN?
YES, MY MIND WAS ELSEWHERE AND SUDDENLY...
AAAAAAAAAAAAAAAAAAAAAAAAA

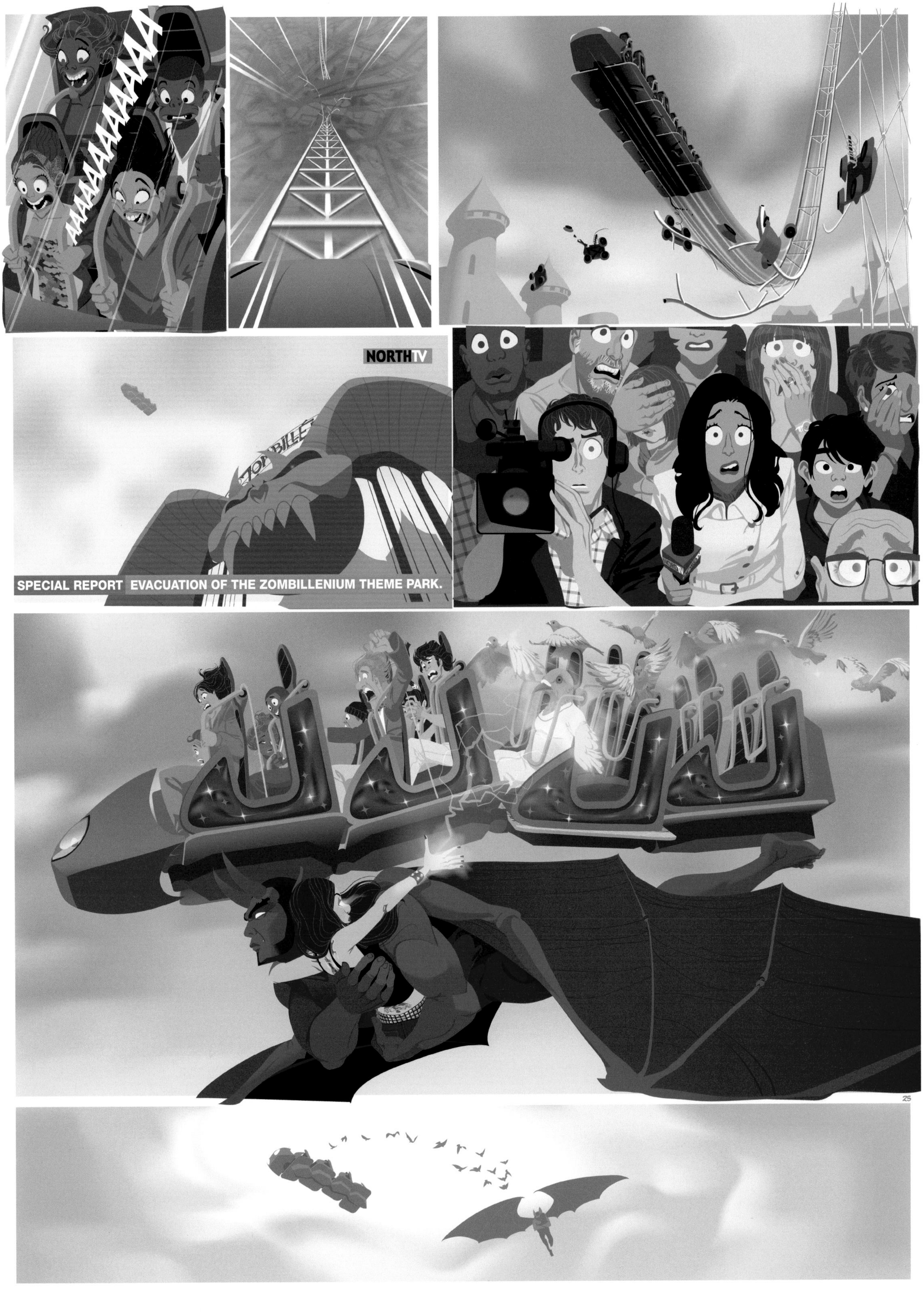
AAAAAAAAAAAAAA
NORTHTV
SPECIAL REPORT EVACUATION OF THE ZOMBILLENIUM THEME PARK.

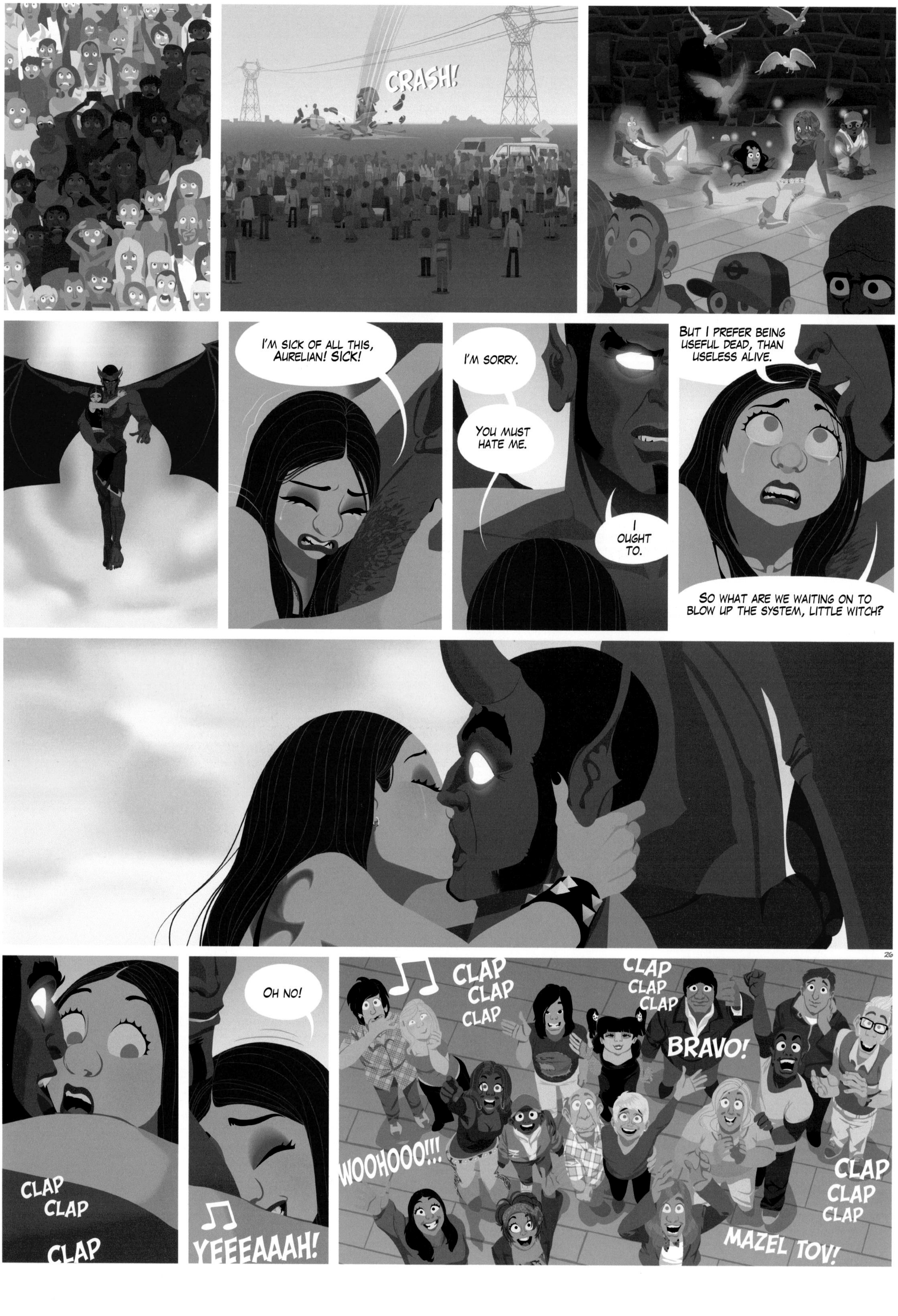
CRASH!
I'M SICK OF ALL THIS, AURELIAN! SICK!
I'M SORRY.
YOU MUST HATE ME.
I OUGHT TO.
BUT I PREFER BEING USEFUL DEAD, THAN USELESS ALIVE.
SO WHAT ARE WE WAITING ON TO BLOW UP THE SYSTEM, LITTLE WITCH?
CLAP CLAP CLAP
OH NO!
YEEEAAAH!
CLAP CLAP CLAP
CLAP CLAP CLAP
BRAVO!
WOOHOOO!!!
CLAP CLAP CLAP
MAZEL TOV!

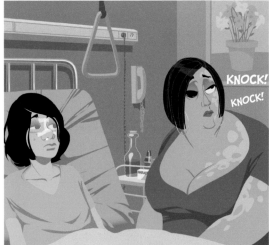

KNOCK!

KNOCK!

HOW'S IT GOING, TIM?

IT'S THE FIRST TIME HE'S BEEN AWAKE SINCE YESTERDAY'S INCIDENT.

I MADE A REAL MESS OF THINGS, HUH?

YES, AND YOU GOT LOTS OF NEW NICKNAMES.

PFFRTT...

"VOMITO," "PUKEFACE," "PIZZAROTH."

PFAA! CLEVER!

AURELIAN, IS IT TRUE WHAT THEY SAY? YOU AND I WERE...

...HIRED FOR A PRODUCTIVITY THING.

BUT THEN, THAT DOESN'T MEAN WE'RE BAD PEOPLE!

YOU REALLY WERE A NASTY PIECE OF WORK, HELEN.

BUT NOBODY DESERVES TO BE IN ZOMBILLENIUM.

BY THE WAY, VOM...

UH, TIM!

YOU HAVE TO TELL US A LITTLE ABOUT WHAT GOT INTO YOU.

THIS MORNING, AT SCHOOL...

I WAS GETTING BULLIED AGAIN BY GREGORY CARON AND HIS CREW.

BAM!

27

OKAY, LET'S SAY THAT THEY'D ALREADY BULLIED ME. THEY'D JUST COME TO TELL ME THEY'D FOUND SOMETHING THEY DIDN'T LIKE IN MY LOCKER, WHICH THEY'D BROKEN INTO.

A LETTER FROM ZOMBILLENIUM, WHAT WAS IT DOING THERE? I DIDN'T KNOW ANY MORE THAN THEY DID! ESPECIALLY SINCE I AVOID THE TOPIC IN SCHOOL...

WHAT'S THIS, TIMBO?

Hell, November 24, 2011

YOU WORK FOR ZOMBILLENIUM?

WELL?

CLUMP!

CLUMP!

THE ONES WHO SENT MY BROTHERS TO JAIL?

I DIDN'T KNOW WHO'D PUT THAT LETTER IN MY LOCKER.

BUT READING IT IMMEDIATELY TELEPORTED ME INTO ASTAROTH'S SKIN, WITH A BURNING DESIRE TO HURT SOMETHING HUMAN.

OKAY, SO WHAT WAS THAT LETTER...

AN INCITEMENT TO MURDER.

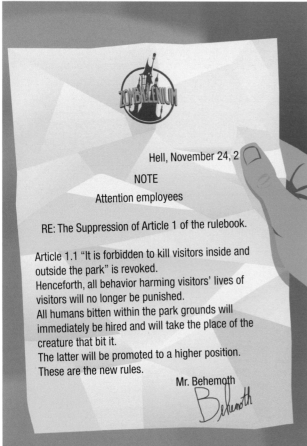

![Zombillenium logo]

Hell, November 24, 2

NOTE

Attention employees

RE: The Suppression of Article 1 of the rulebook.

Article 1.1 "It is forbidden to kill visitors inside and outside the park" is revoked.
Henceforth, all behavior harming visitors' lives of visitors will no longer be punished.
All humans bitten within the park grounds will immediately be hired and will take the place of the creature that bit it.
The latter will be promoted to a higher position.
These are the new rules.

Mr. Behemoth

Behemoth

IT'S SIGNED BEHEMOTH?

I'D BET KATE MIDDLETON'S UNDIES IT'S JAGGAR WHO SIGNED IT.

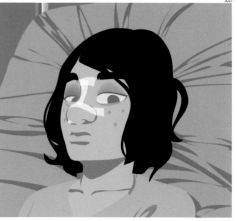

JUST WHAT IS THAT GUY AFTER? CLOSING DOWN THE PARK?

I'LL GO SEE IF THE OTHER EMPLOYEES GOT THE SAME LETTER.

28

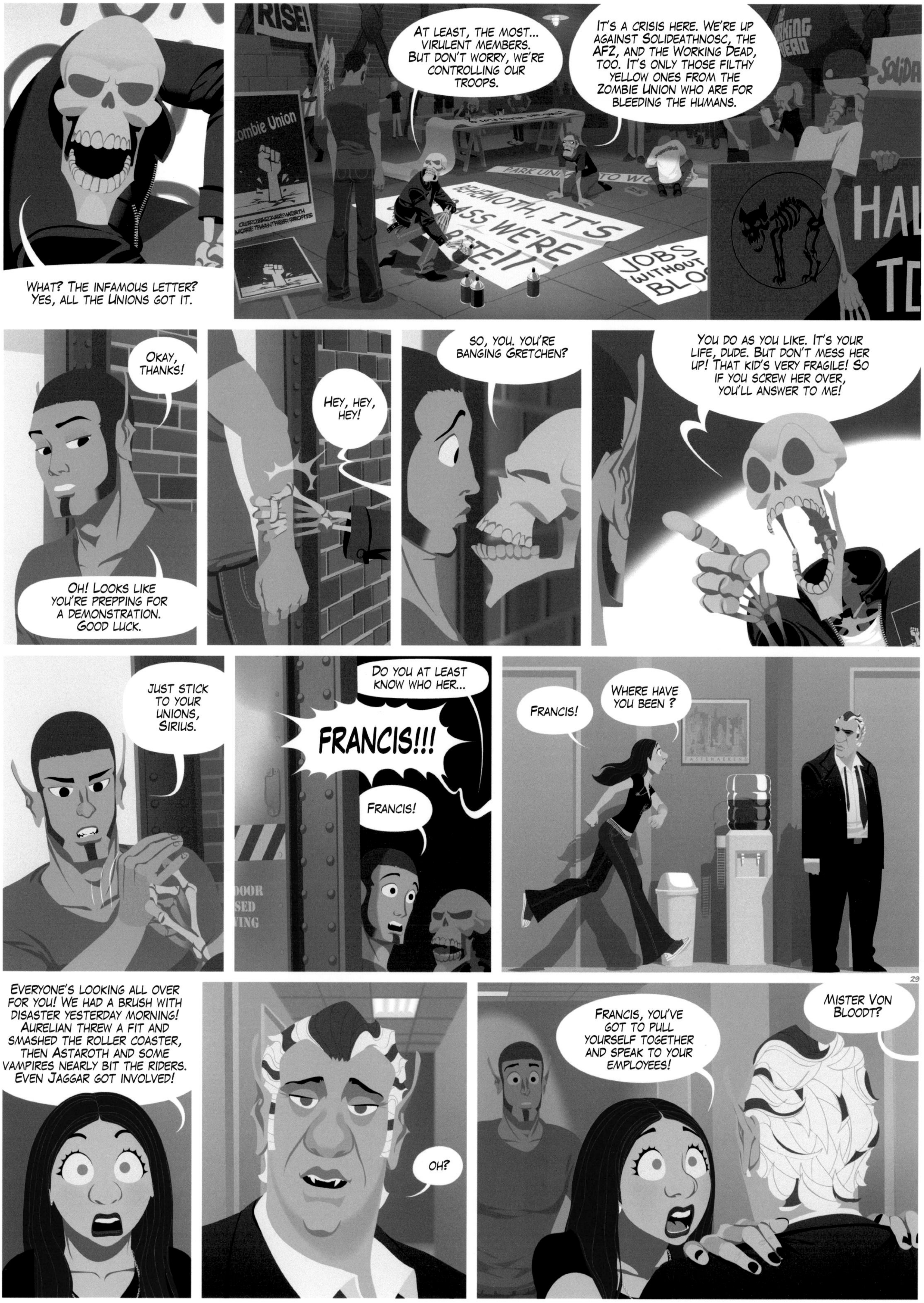

What? The infamous letter? Yes, all the Unions got it.
RISE!
Zombie Union
At least, the most... virulent members. But don't worry, we're controlling our troops.
It's a crisis here. We're up against Solideathnosc, the AFZ, and the Working Dead, too. It's only those filthy yellow ones from the Zombie Union who are for bleeding the humans.
Okay, thanks!
Oh! Looks like you're prepping for a demonstration. Good luck.
Hey, hey, hey!
So, you. You're banging Gretchen?
You do as you like. It's your life, dude. But don't mess her up! That kid's very fragile! So if you screw her over, you'll answer to me!
Just stick to your unions, Sirius.
Do you at least know who her...
FRANCIS!!!
Francis!
Francis!
Where have you been ?
Everyone's looking all over for you! We had a brush with disaster yesterday morning! Aurelian threw a fit and smashed the roller coaster, then Astaroth and some vampires nearly bit the riders. Even Jaggar got involved!
Oh?
Francis, you've got to pull yourself together and speak to your employees!
Mister Von Bloodt?

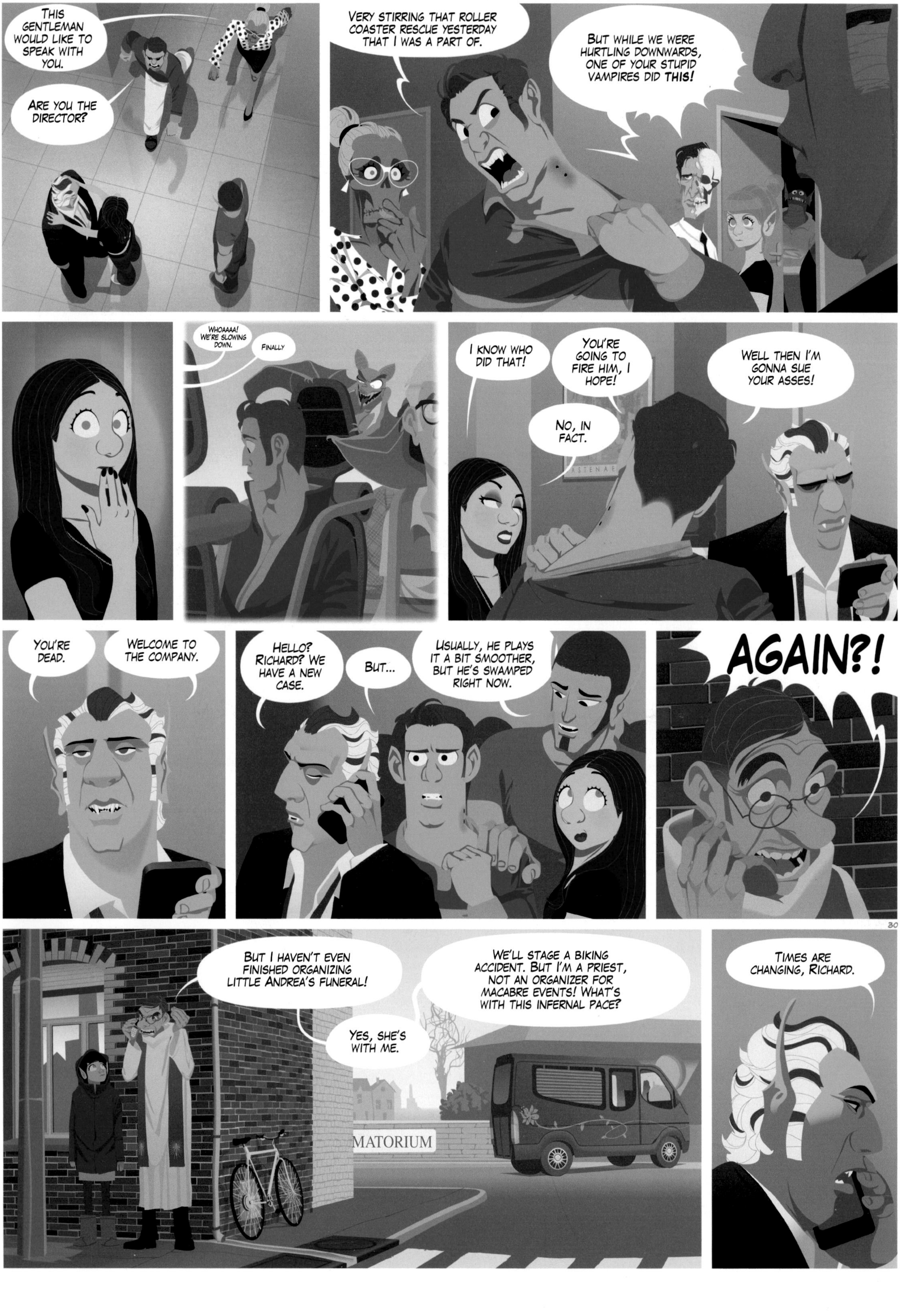
THIS GENTLEMAN WOULD LIKE TO SPEAK WITH YOU.
ARE YOU THE DIRECTOR?
VERY STIRRING THAT ROLLER COASTER RESCUE YESTERDAY THAT I WAS A PART OF.
BUT WHILE WE WERE HURTLING DOWNWARDS, ONE OF YOUR STUPID VAMPIRES DID THIS!
WHOAAAA! WE'RE SLOWING DOWN.
FINALLY
I KNOW WHO DID THAT!
YOU'RE GOING TO FIRE HIM, I HOPE!
NO, IN FACT.
WELL THEN I'M GONNA SUE YOUR ASSES!
YOU'RE DEAD.
WELCOME TO THE COMPANY.
HELLO? RICHARD? WE HAVE A NEW CASE.
BUT...
USUALLY, HE PLAYS IT A BIT SMOOTHER, BUT HE'S SWAMPED RIGHT NOW.
AGAIN?!
BUT I HAVEN'T EVEN FINISHED ORGANIZING LITTLE ANDREA'S FUNERAL!
YES, SHE'S WITH ME.
WE'LL STAGE A BIKING ACCIDENT. BUT I'M A PRIEST, NOT AN ORGANIZER FOR MACABRE EVENTS! WHAT'S WITH THIS INFERNAL PACE?
MATORIUM
TIMES ARE CHANGING, RICHARD.

WE DIDN'T KNOW IF IT WAS REAL OR NOT, TO TELL YOU THE TRUTH.

SPECIAL REPORT EVACUATION OF THE ZOMBILLENIUM THEME PARK.

WERE YOU AFRAID?

EVACUATION OF THE ZOMBILLENIUM THEME PARK.

YEAH, BUT IT WAS AWESOME!

VATION OF THE ZOMBILLENIUM THEME

CLICK!

DO ANY OF YOU STILL HAVE ANY DOUBTS CONCERNING THE PUBLICITY SURROUNDING THE PARK?

UH, NOPE!

NICE MARKETING STUNT, BY THE WAY.

YES, GIVEN THE CROWDS AFTER THE REOPENING, WE CAN SAY IT WORKED!

AND AFTER ALL, NOBODY MADE ANY COMPLAINTS.

NIUM

CORD
ROWDS

a week that the
amusement park
billenium closed
oors because of
ation of maintenance
ecutive signaling
defective attraction.
He latter had
ntioned the evacuation of
last week.
we'd have to believe the
ctos of the park are
sorcerers to have succeeded
transforming this
cident into
cellent publicity stunt.
e should believe
anagement,
ing was under control.
he rollercoaster passengers
knowingly experienced
ur new amusement
From now on, at

The park reopens its doors.

MORMONT-ON-DEADMAN

Two fatal bicycle accidents over a three-day span

Is the roundabout at the intersection of D88 and the D40A cursed? Only three days after the tragic fall from a bicycle which cost the young Andrea C. her life, a new case of a fatal fall occurred at that same roundabout located at the entrance to the city.

Ordinarily, the two victims never rode bicycles.

The circumstances, however aren't the same. Whereas the first victim fell on a curb, the second, according to the results of the investigation, skidded on a pile of dead leaves.

These two tragic events, which have plunged the community and its surroundings into mourning ha reopened the debate on the safe of bicycle users.
All the same, nobody can explai the reasons for these two incid the pavement is practically ne the hole had been filled the evening before and dead leav are rare during this season.

MISTER JAGGAR, THIS EVENT HAS BEEN QUITE COSTLY. WILL WE HAVE TO REBUILD A ROLLER COASTER EVERY DAY?

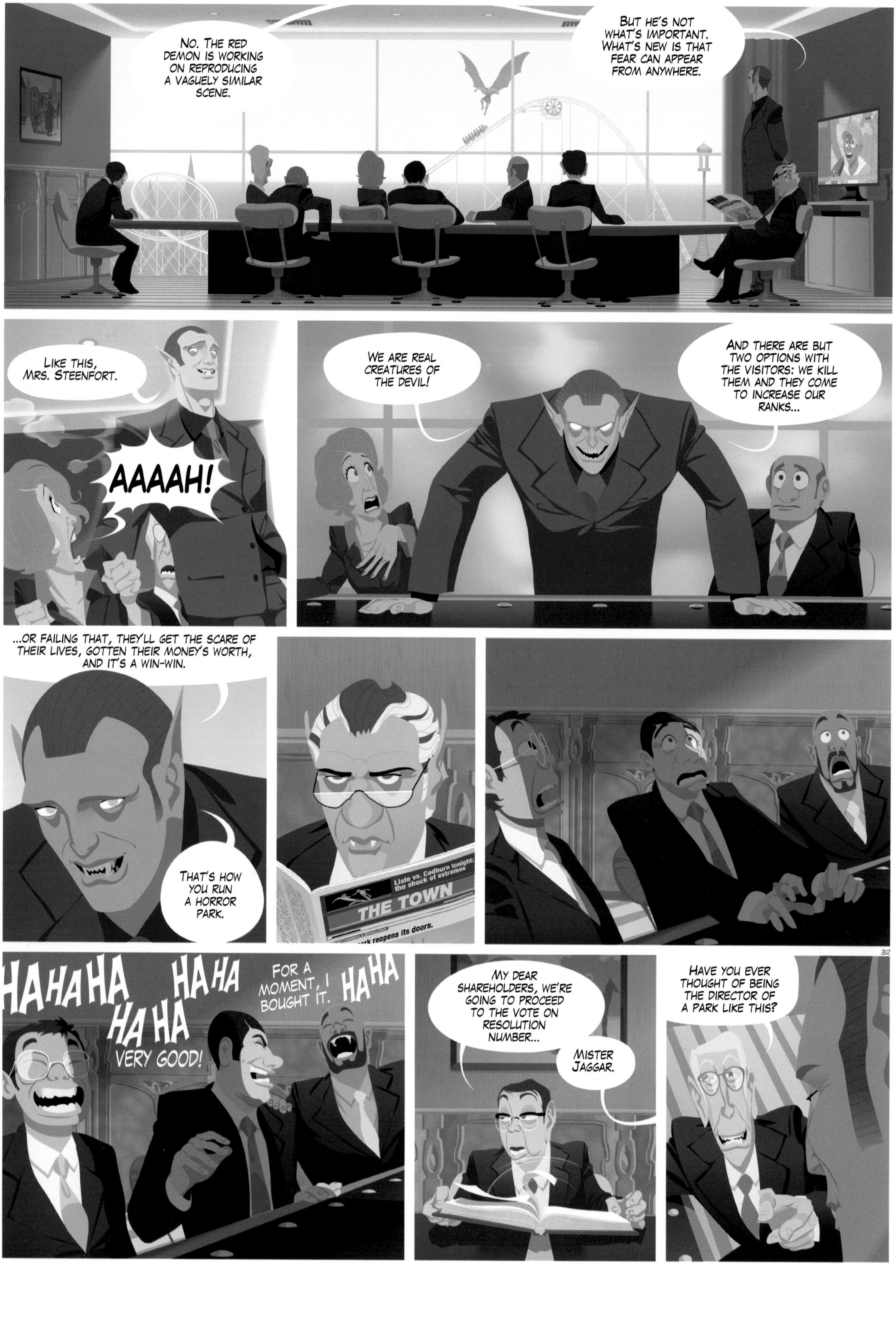
No. The red demon is working on reproducing a vaguely similar scene.
But he's not what's important. What's new is that fear can appear from anywhere.
Like this, Mrs. Steenfort.
AAAAH!
We are real creatures of the devil!
And there are but two options with the visitors: we kill them and they come to increase our ranks...
...or failing that, they'll get the scare of their lives, gotten their money's worth, and it's a win-win.
That's how you run a horror park.
Lisle vs. Cadburn tonight: the shock of extremes
THE TOWN
reopens its doors.
HAHAHA HAHA HAHA
VERY GOOD!
For a moment, I bought it.
HAHA
My dear shareholders, we're going to proceed to the vote on resolution number...
Mister Jaggar.
Have you ever thought of being the director of a park like this?

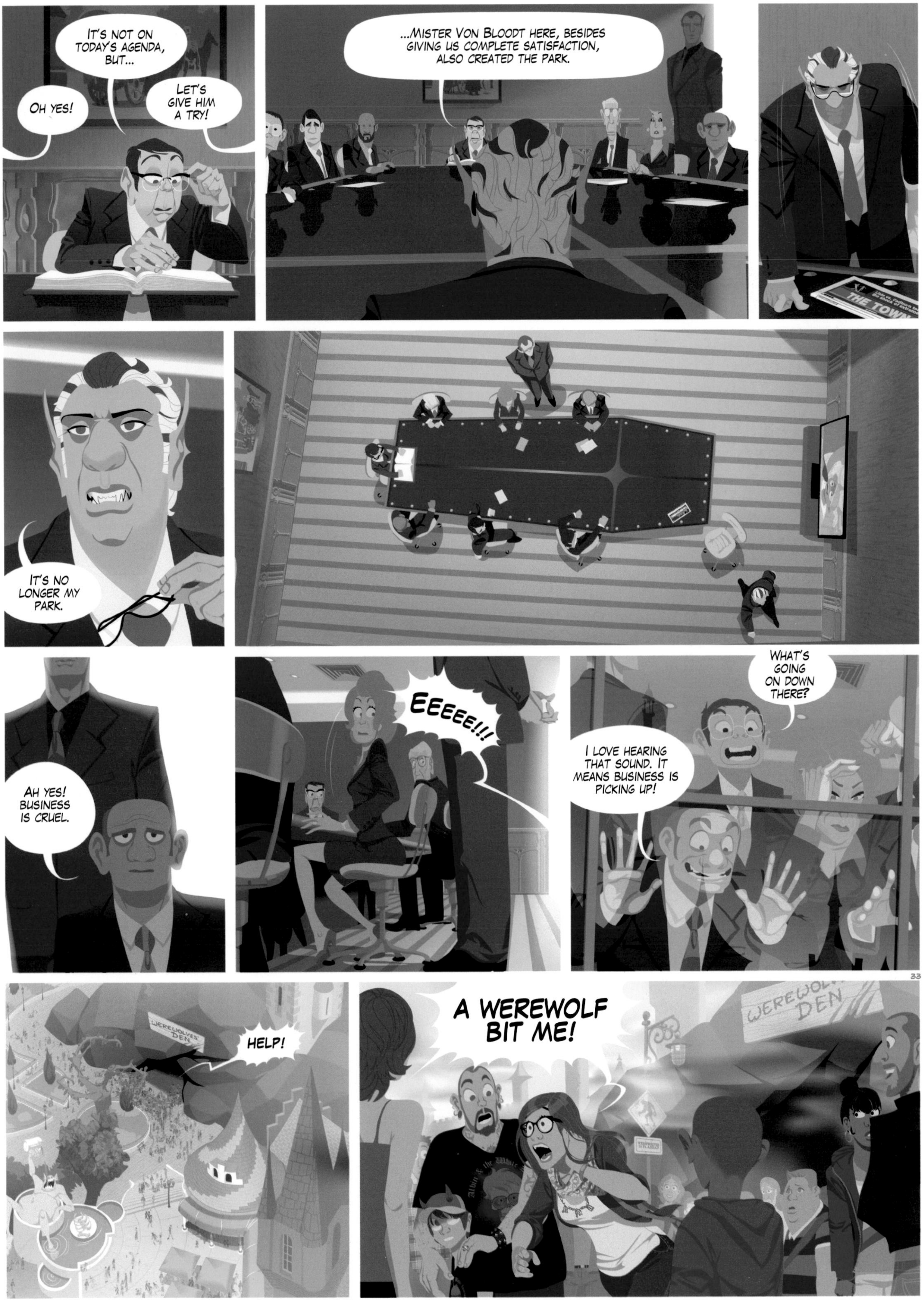
IT'S NOT ON TODAY'S AGENDA, BUT...
OH YES!
LET'S GIVE HIM A TRY!
...MISTER VON BLOODT HERE, BESIDES GIVING US COMPLETE SATISFACTION, ALSO CREATED THE PARK.
IT'S NO LONGER MY PARK.
AH YES! BUSINESS IS CRUEL.
EEEEE!!!
WHAT'S GOING ON DOWN THERE?
I LOVE HEARING THAT SOUND. IT MEANS BUSINESS IS PICKING UP!
WEREWOLVES' DEN
HELP!
A WEREWOLF BIT ME!

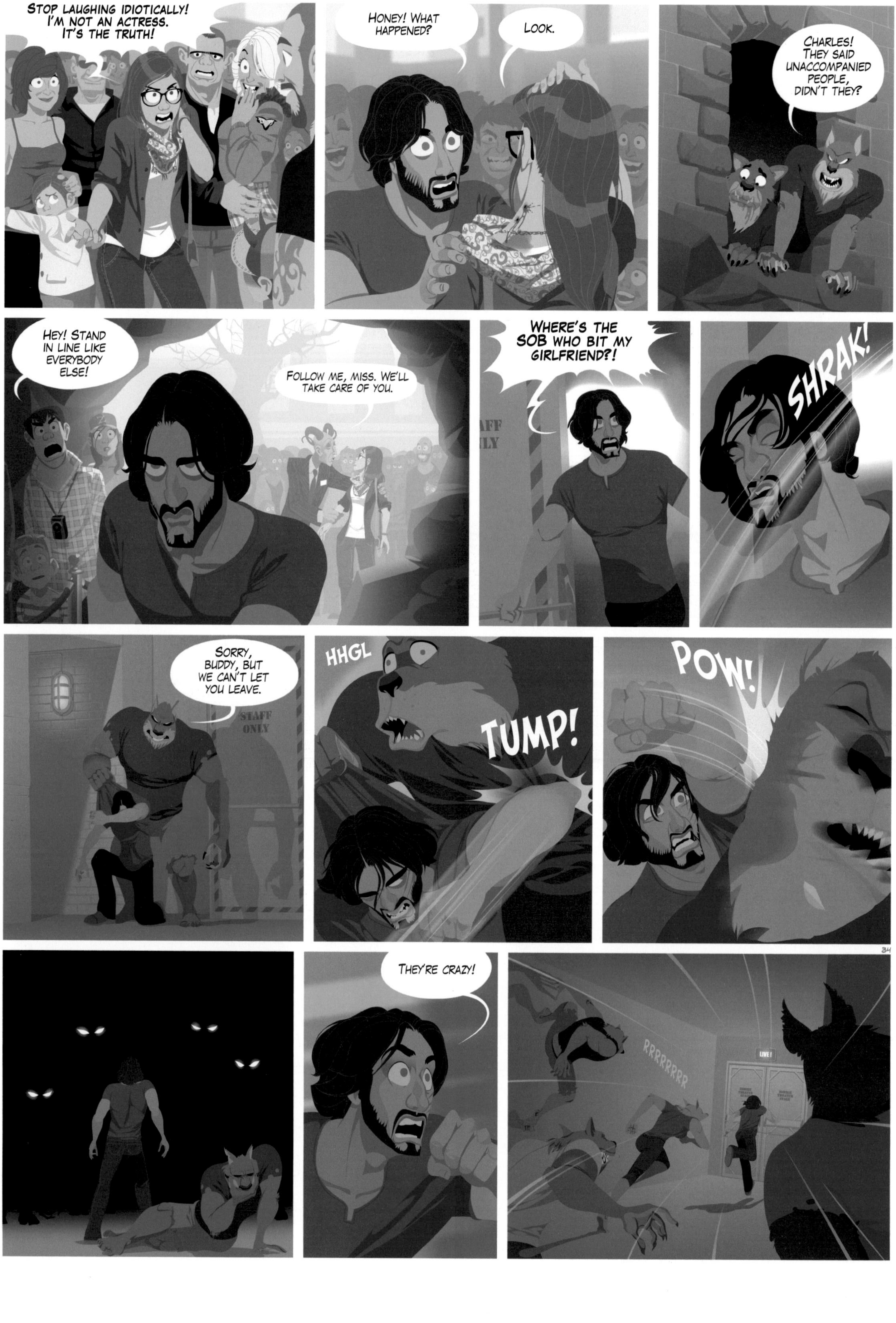
STOP LAUGHING IDIOTICALLY! I'M NOT AN ACTRESS. IT'S THE TRUTH!
HONEY! WHAT HAPPENED?
LOOK.
CHARLES! THEY SAID UNACCOMPANIED PEOPLE, DIDN'T THEY?
HEY! STAND IN LINE LIKE EVERYBODY ELSE!
FOLLOW ME, MISS. WE'LL TAKE CARE OF YOU.
WHERE'S THE SOB WHO BIT MY GIRLFRIEND?!
SHRAK!
SORRY, BUDDY, BUT WE CAN'T LET YOU LEAVE.
STAFF ONLY
HHGL
TUMP!
POW!
THEY'RE CRAZY!
RRRRRRRR
LIVE!

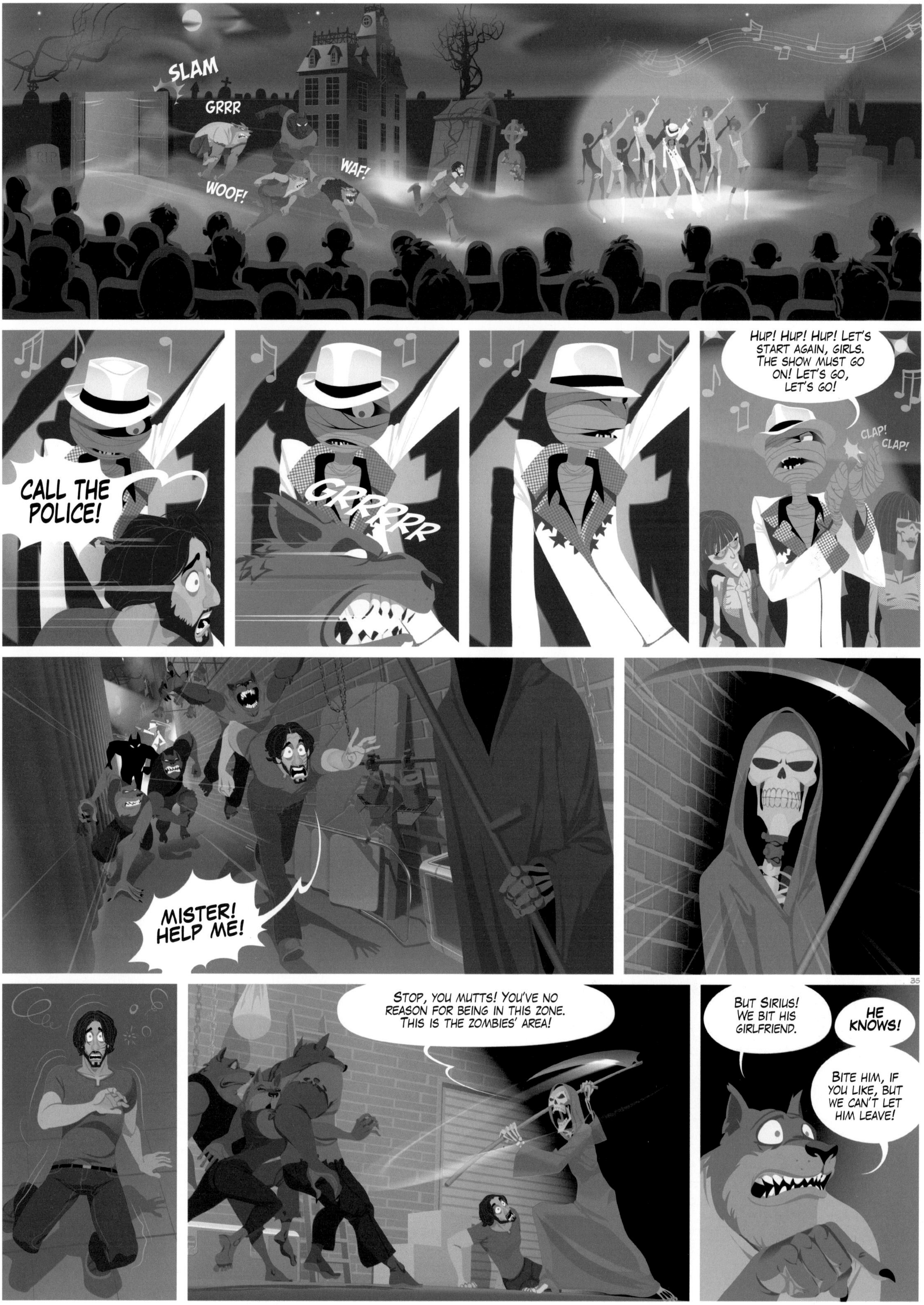
SLAM
GRRR
WAF!
WOOF!
CALL THE POLICE!
GRRRRR
HUP! HUP! HUP! LET'S START AGAIN, GIRLS. THE SHOW MUST GO ON! LET'S GO, LET'S GO!
CLAP!
CLAP!
MISTER! HELP ME!
STOP, YOU MUTTS! YOU'VE NO REASON FOR BEING IN THIS ZONE. THIS IS THE ZOMBIES' AREA!
BUT SIRIUS! WE BIT HIS GIRLFRIEND.
HE KNOWS!
BITE HIM, IF YOU LIKE, BUT WE CAN'T LET HIM LEAVE!

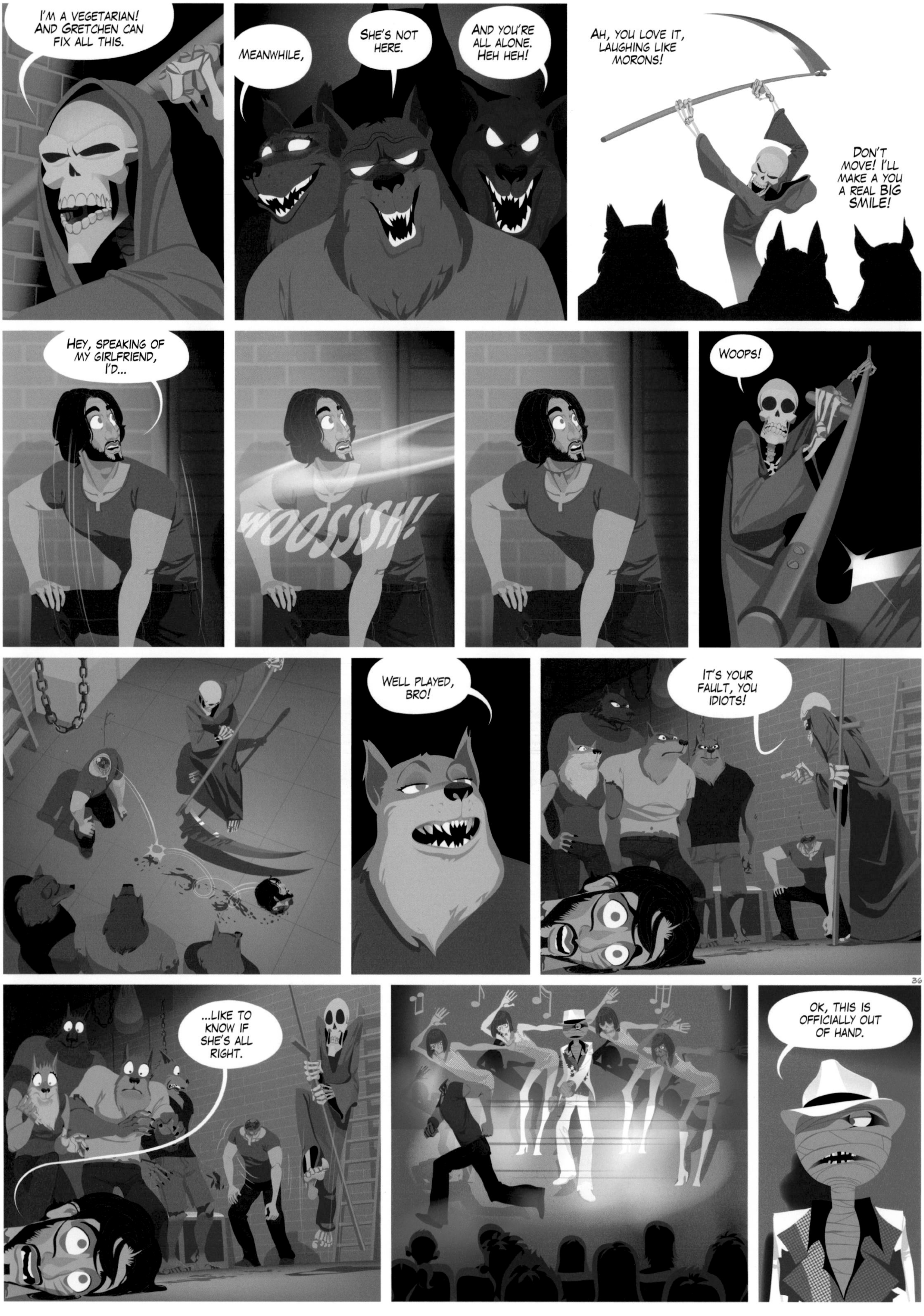
I'M A VEGETARIAN! AND GRETCHEN CAN FIX ALL THIS.
MEANWHILE,
SHE'S NOT HERE.
AND YOU'RE ALL ALONE. HEH HEH!
AH, YOU LOVE IT, LAUGHING LIKE MORONS!
DON'T MOVE! I'LL MAKE A YOU A REAL BIG SMILE!
HEY, SPEAKING OF MY GIRLFRIEND, I'D...
WOOSSSH!
WOOPS!
WELL PLAYED, BRO!
IT'S YOUR FAULT, YOU IDIOTS!
...LIKE TO KNOW IF SHE'S ALL RIGHT.
OK, THIS IS OFFICIALLY OUT OF HAND.

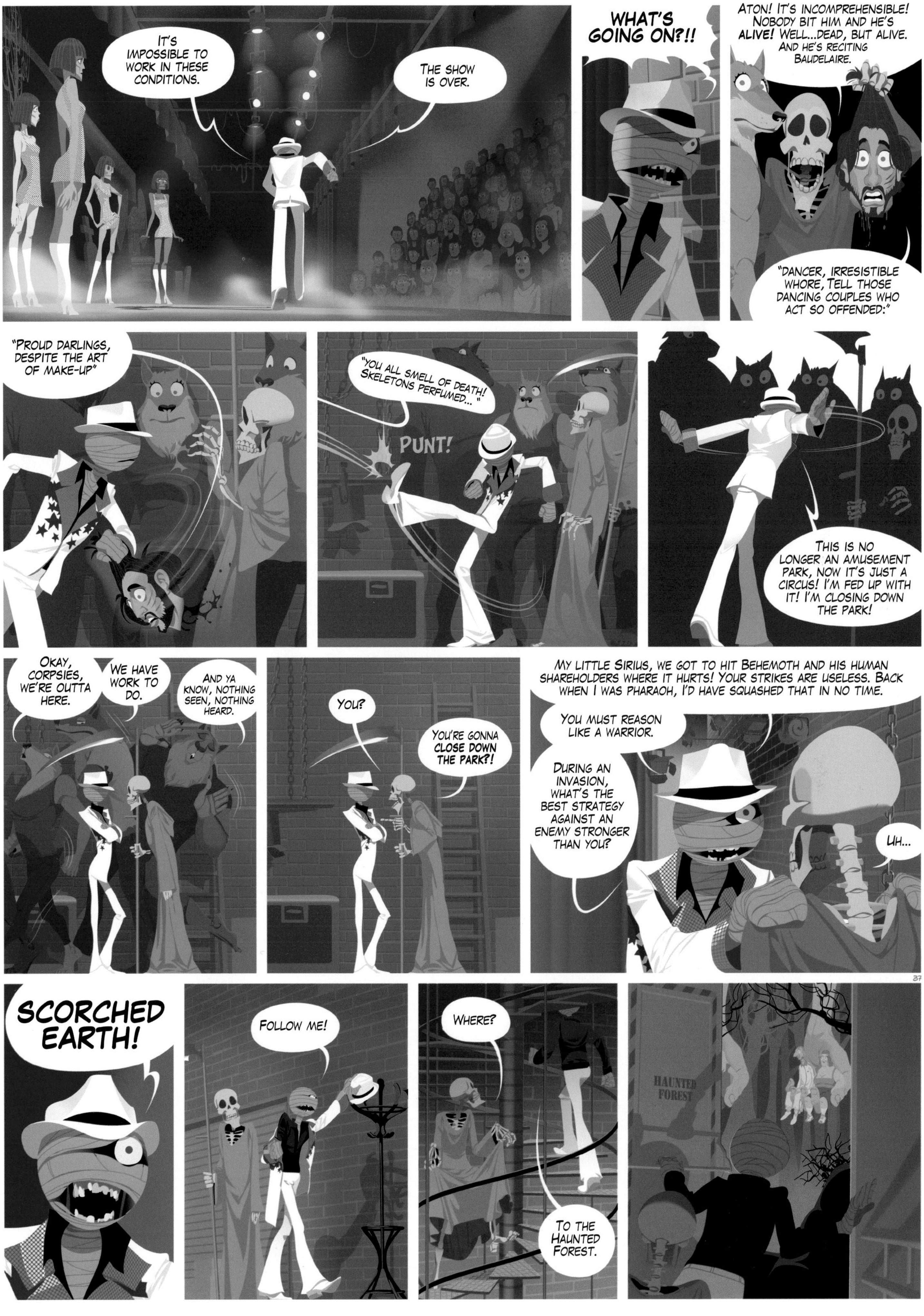

It's impossible to work in these conditions.
The show is over.
What's going on?!!
Aton! It's incomprehensible! Nobody bit him and he's alive! Well...dead, but alive. And he's reciting Baudelaire.
"Dancer, irresistible whore, Tell those dancing couples who act so offended:"
"Proud darlings, despite the art of make-up"
"You all smell of death! Skeletons perfumed..."
PUNT!
This is no longer an amusement park, now it's just a circus! I'm fed up with it! I'm closing down the park!
Okay, corpsies, we're outta here.
We have work to do.
And ya know, nothing seen, nothing heard.
You?
You're gonna close down the park?!
My little Sirius, we got to hit Behemoth and his human shareholders where it hurts! Your strikes are useless. Back when I was pharaoh, I'd have squashed that in no time.
You must reason like a warrior.
During an invasion, what's the best strategy against an enemy stronger than you?
Uh...
37
Scorched earth!
Follow me!
Where?
To the Haunted Forest.
Haunted Forest

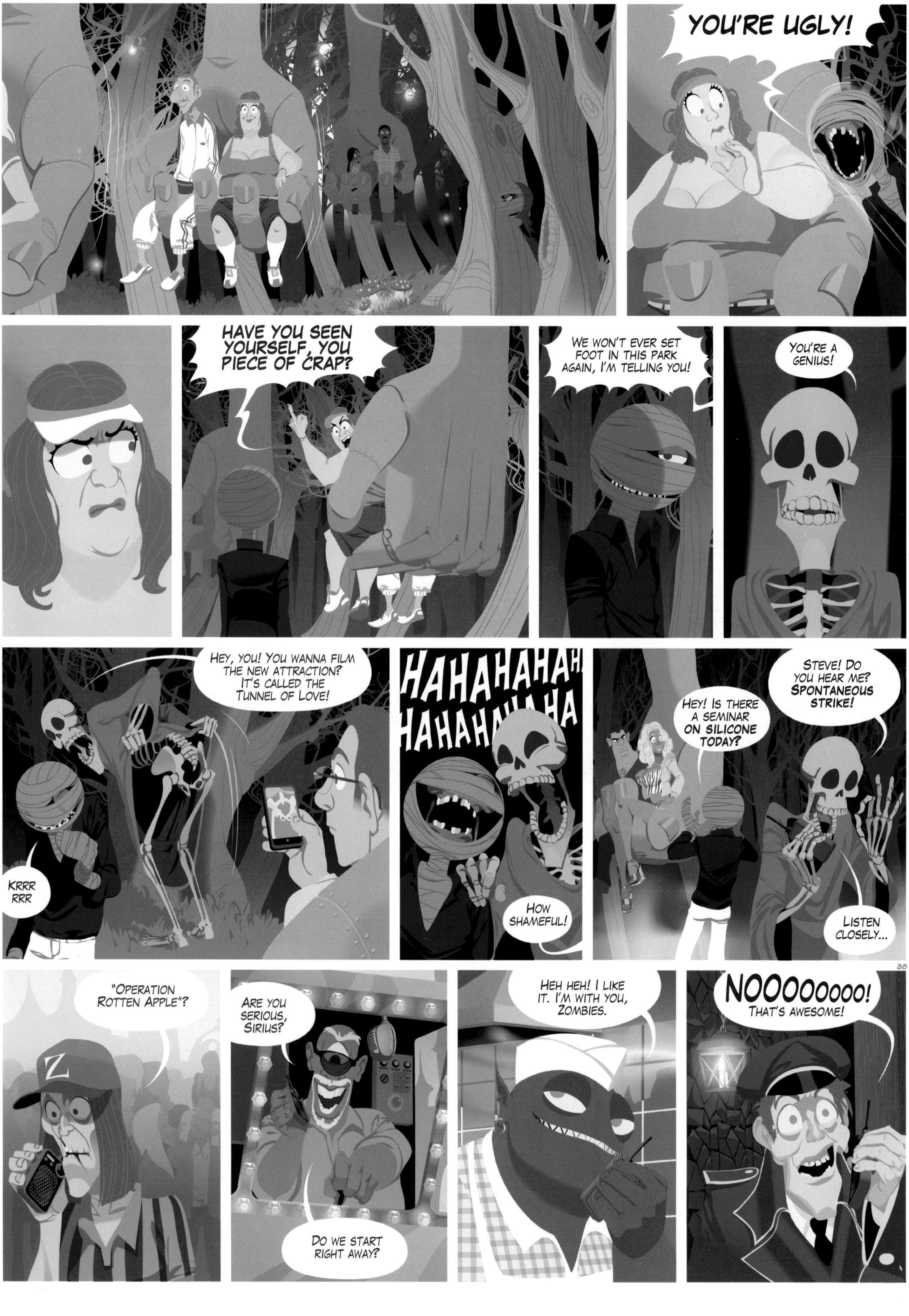
YOU'RE UGLY!
HAVE YOU SEEN YOURSELF, YOU PIECE OF CRAP?
WE WON'T EVER SET FOOT IN THIS PARK AGAIN, I'M TELLING YOU!
YOU'RE A GENIUS!
HEY, YOU! YOU WANNA FILM THE NEW ATTRACTION? IT'S CALLED THE TUNNEL OF LOVE!
KRRR RRR
HAHAHAHAH HAHAHAHAHA
HOW SHAMEFUL!
HEY! IS THERE A SEMINAR ON SILICONE TODAY?
STEVE! DO YOU HEAR ME? SPONTANEOUS STRIKE!
LISTEN CLOSELY...
"OPERATION ROTTEN APPLE"?
ARE YOU SERIOUS, SIRIUS?
DO WE START RIGHT AWAY?
HEH HEH! I LIKE IT. I'M WITH YOU, ZOMBIES.
NOOOOOOOO! THAT'S AWESOME!

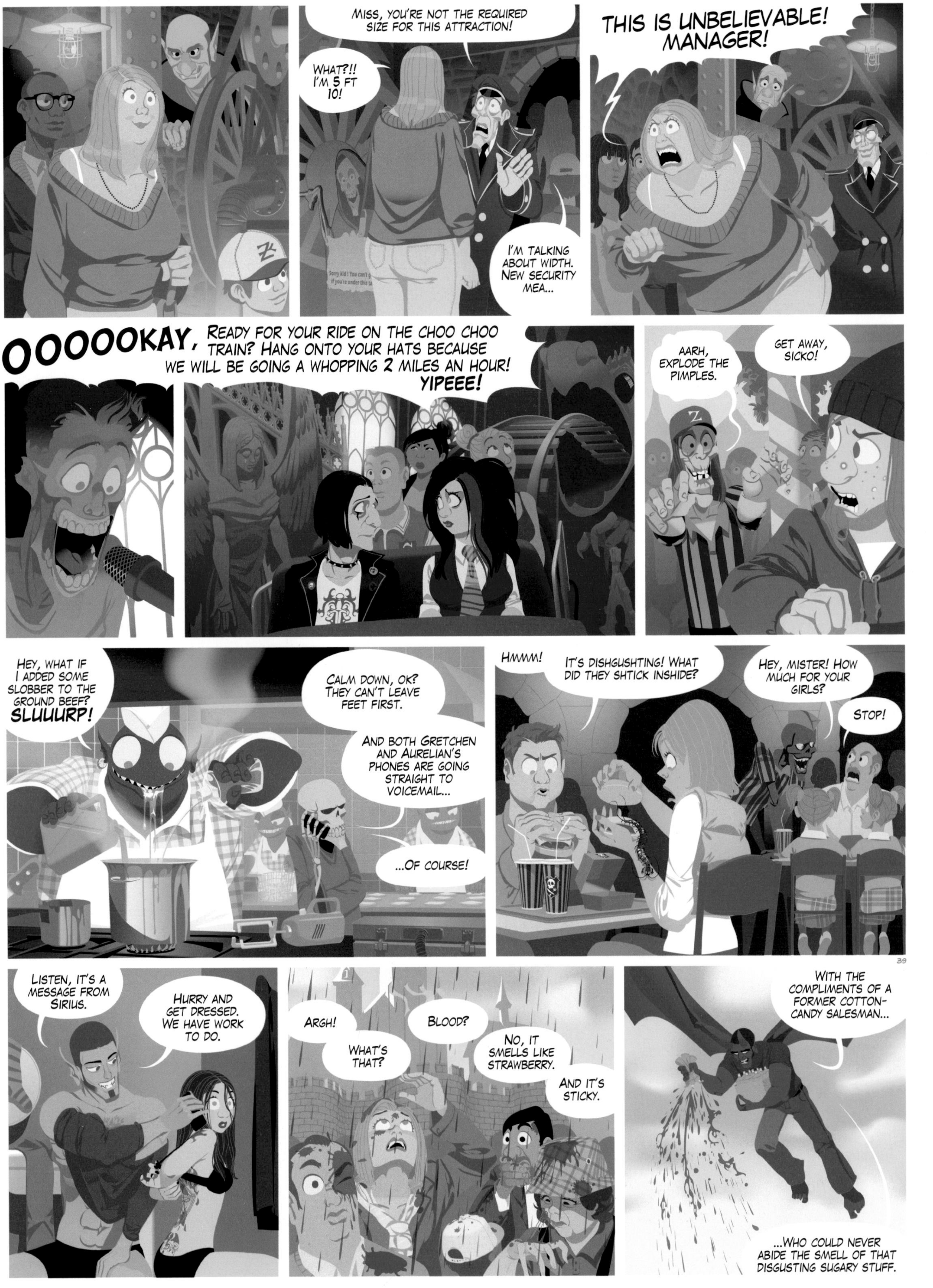

MISS, YOU'RE NOT THE REQUIRED SIZE FOR THIS ATTRACTION!
WHAT?!! I'M 5 FT 10!
I'M TALKING ABOUT WIDTH. NEW SECURITY MEA...
THIS IS UNBELIEVABLE! MANAGER!
OOOOOKAY, READY FOR YOUR RIDE ON THE CHOO CHOO TRAIN? HANG ONTO YOUR HATS BECAUSE WE WILL BE GOING A WHOPPING 2 MILES AN HOUR! YIPEEE!
AARH, EXPLODE THE PIMPLES.
GET AWAY, SICKO!
HEY, WHAT IF I ADDED SOME SLOBBER TO THE GROUND BEEF? SLUUURP!
CALM DOWN, OK? THEY CAN'T LEAVE FEET FIRST.
AND BOTH GRETCHEN AND AURELIAN'S PHONES ARE GOING STRAIGHT TO VOICEMAIL...
...OF COURSE!
HMMM!
IT'S DISHGUSHTING! WHAT DID THEY SHTICK INSHIDE?
HEY, MISTER! HOW MUCH FOR YOUR GIRLS?
STOP!
LISTEN, IT'S A MESSAGE FROM SIRIUS.
HURRY AND GET DRESSED. WE HAVE WORK TO DO.
ARGH!
BLOOD?
WHAT'S THAT?
NO, IT SMELLS LIKE STRAWBERRY.
AND IT'S STICKY.
WITH THE COMPLIMENTS OF A FORMER COTTON-CANDY SALESMAN...
...WHO COULD NEVER ABIDE THE SMELL OF THAT DISGUSTING SUGARY STUFF.

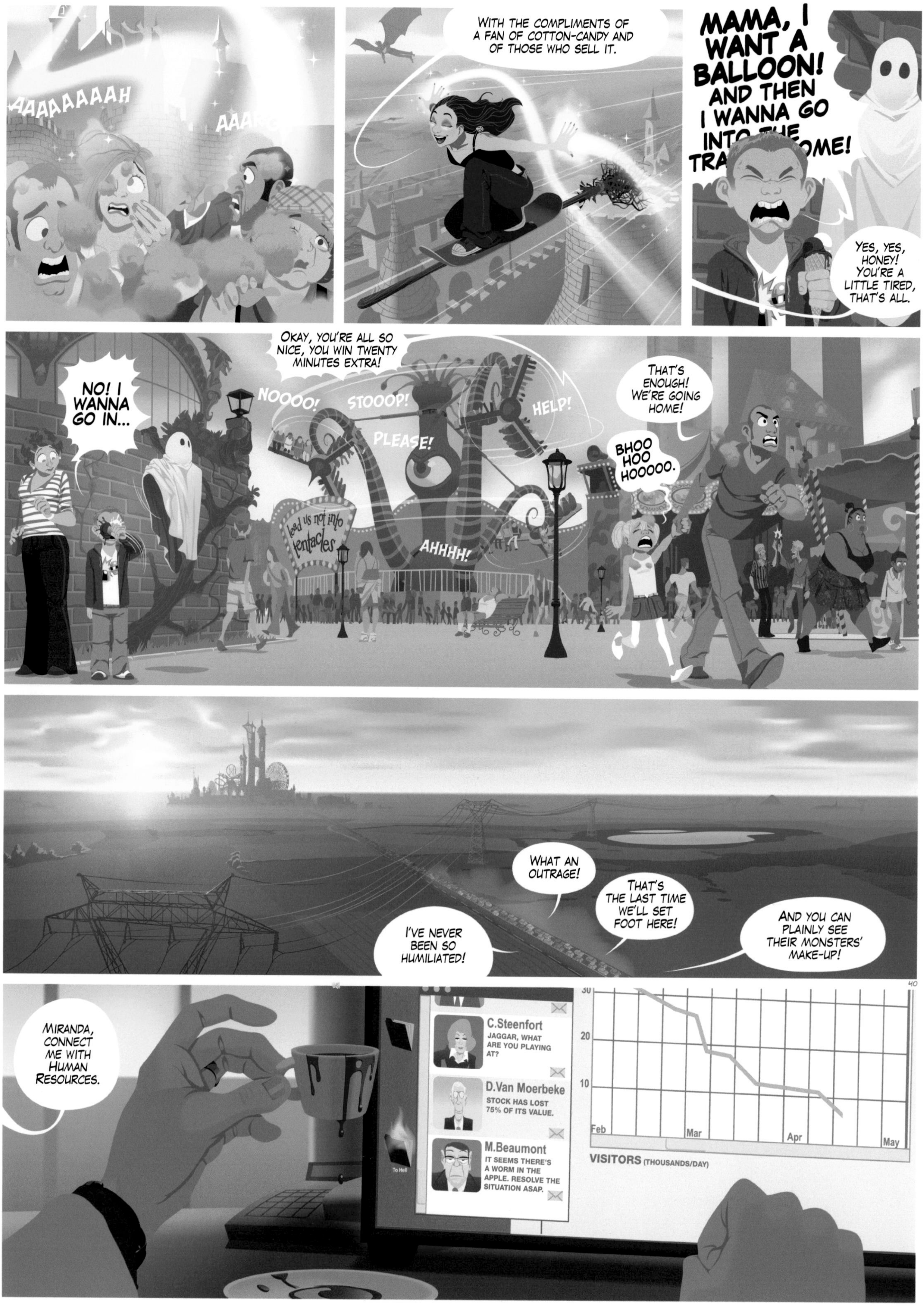
AAAAAAAAH
AAARG
WITH THE COMPLIMENTS OF A FAN OF COTTON-CANDY AND OF THOSE WHO SELL IT.
MAMA, I WANT A BALLOON! AND THEN I WANNA GO INTO THE
YES, YES, HONEY! YOU'RE A LITTLE TIRED, THAT'S ALL.
NO! I WANNA GO IN...
OKAY, YOU'RE ALL SO NICE, YOU WIN TWENTY MINUTES EXTRA!
NOOOO!
STOOOP!
HELP!
PLEASE!
lead us not into tentacles
AHHHH!
THAT'S ENOUGH! WE'RE GOING HOME!
BHOO HOO HOOOOO.
WHAT AN OUTRAGE!
THAT'S THE LAST TIME WE'LL SET FOOT HERE!
I'VE NEVER BEEN SO HUMILIATED!
AND YOU CAN PLAINLY SEE THEIR MONSTERS' MAKE-UP!
MIRANDA, CONNECT ME WITH HUMAN RESOURCES.
C.Steenfort
JAGGAR, WHAT ARE YOU PLAYING AT?
D.Van Moerbeke
STOCK HAS LOST 75% OF ITS VALUE.
M.Beaumont
IT SEEMS THERE'S A WORM IN THE APPLE. RESOLVE THE SITUATION ASAP.
To Hell
30
20
10
Feb
Mar
Apr
May
VISITORS (THOUSANDS/DAY)

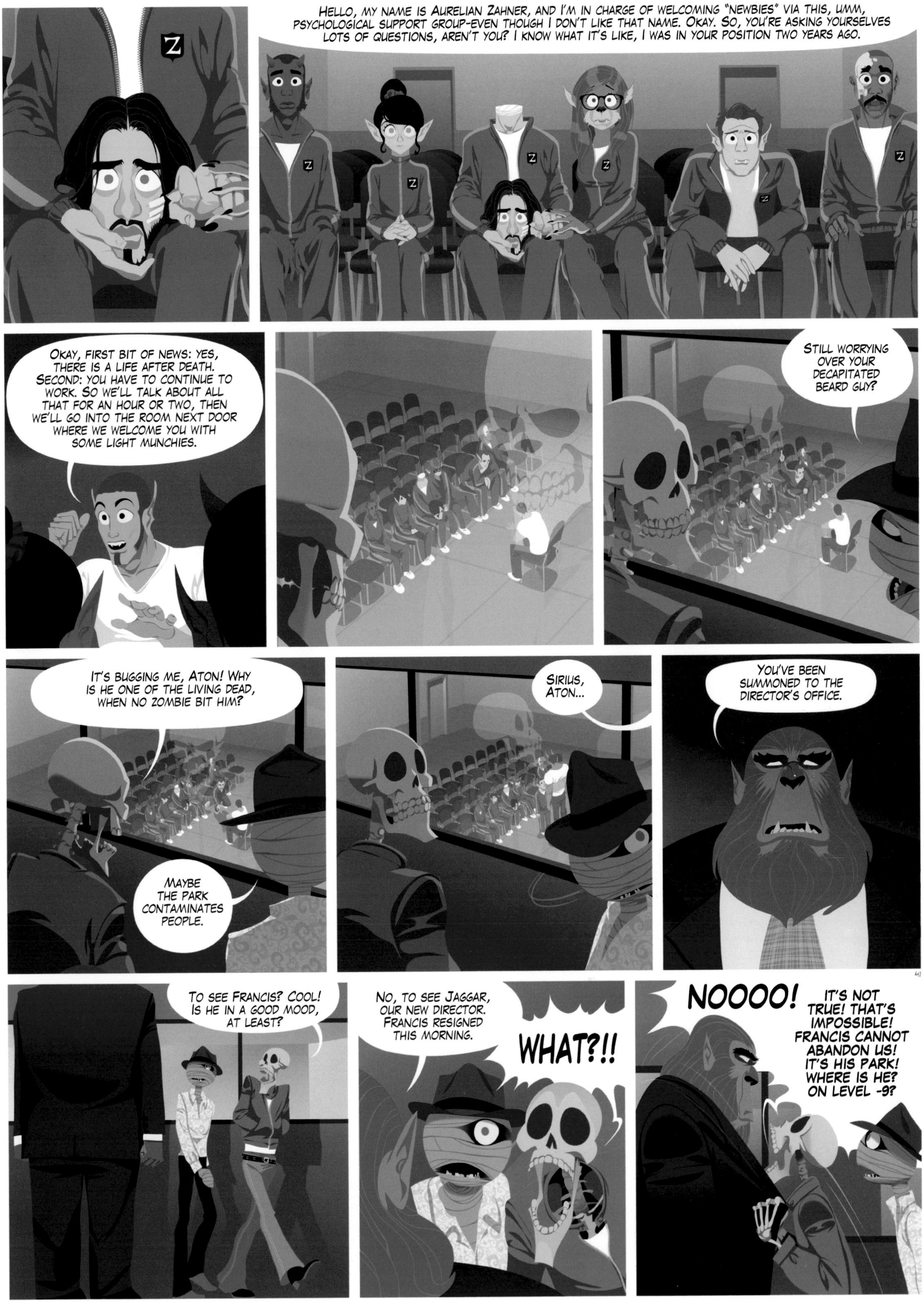
HELLO, MY NAME IS AURELIAN ZAHNER, AND I'M IN CHARGE OF WELCOMING "NEWBIES" VIA THIS, UMM, PSYCHOLOGICAL SUPPORT GROUP-EVEN THOUGH I DON'T LIKE THAT NAME. OKAY. SO, YOU'RE ASKING YOURSELVES LOTS OF QUESTIONS, AREN'T YOU? I KNOW WHAT IT'S LIKE, I WAS IN YOUR POSITION TWO YEARS AGO.
OKAY, FIRST BIT OF NEWS: YES, THERE IS A LIFE AFTER DEATH. SECOND: YOU HAVE TO CONTINUE TO WORK. SO WE'LL TALK ABOUT ALL THAT FOR AN HOUR OR TWO, THEN WE'LL GO INTO THE ROOM NEXT DOOR WHERE WE WELCOME YOU WITH SOME LIGHT MUNCHIES.
STILL WORRYING OVER YOUR DECAPITATED BEARD GUY?
IT'S BUGGING ME, ATON! WHY IS HE ONE OF THE LIVING DEAD, WHEN NO ZOMBIE BIT HIM?
MAYBE THE PARK CONTAMINATES PEOPLE.
SIRIUS, ATON...
YOU'VE BEEN SUMMONED TO THE DIRECTOR'S OFFICE.
TO SEE FRANCIS? COOL! IS HE IN A GOOD MOOD, AT LEAST?
NO, TO SEE JAGGAR, OUR NEW DIRECTOR. FRANCIS RESIGNED THIS MORNING.
WHAT?!!
NOOOO!
IT'S NOT TRUE! THAT'S IMPOSSIBLE! FRANCIS CANNOT ABANDON US! IT'S HIS PARK! WHERE IS HE? ON LEVEL -9?

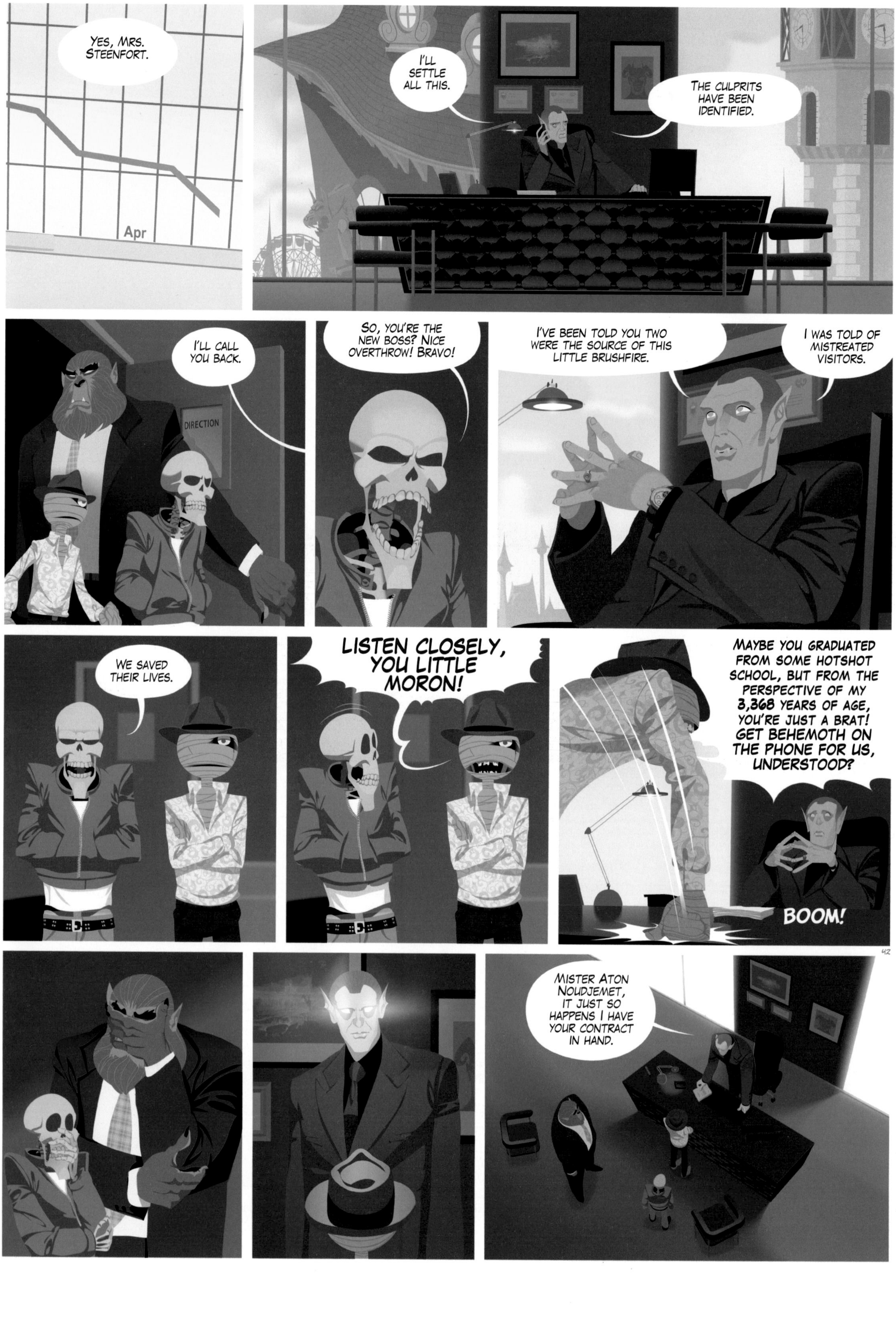

YES, MRS. STEENFORT.
Apr
I'LL SETTLE ALL THIS.
THE CULPRITS HAVE BEEN IDENTIFIED.
I'LL CALL YOU BACK.
DIRECTION
SO, YOU'RE THE NEW BOSS? NICE OVERTHROW! BRAVO!
I'VE BEEN TOLD YOU TWO WERE THE SOURCE OF THIS LITTLE BRUSHFIRE.
I WAS TOLD OF MISTREATED VISITORS.
WE SAVED THEIR LIVES.
LISTEN CLOSELY, YOU LITTLE MORON!
MAYBE YOU GRADUATED FROM SOME HOTSHOT SCHOOL, BUT FROM THE PERSPECTIVE OF MY 3,368 YEARS OF AGE, YOU'RE JUST A BRAT! GET BEHEMOTH ON THE PHONE FOR US, UNDERSTOOD?
BOOM!
MISTER ATON NOUDJEMET, IT JUST SO HAPPENS I HAVE YOUR CONTRACT IN HAND.

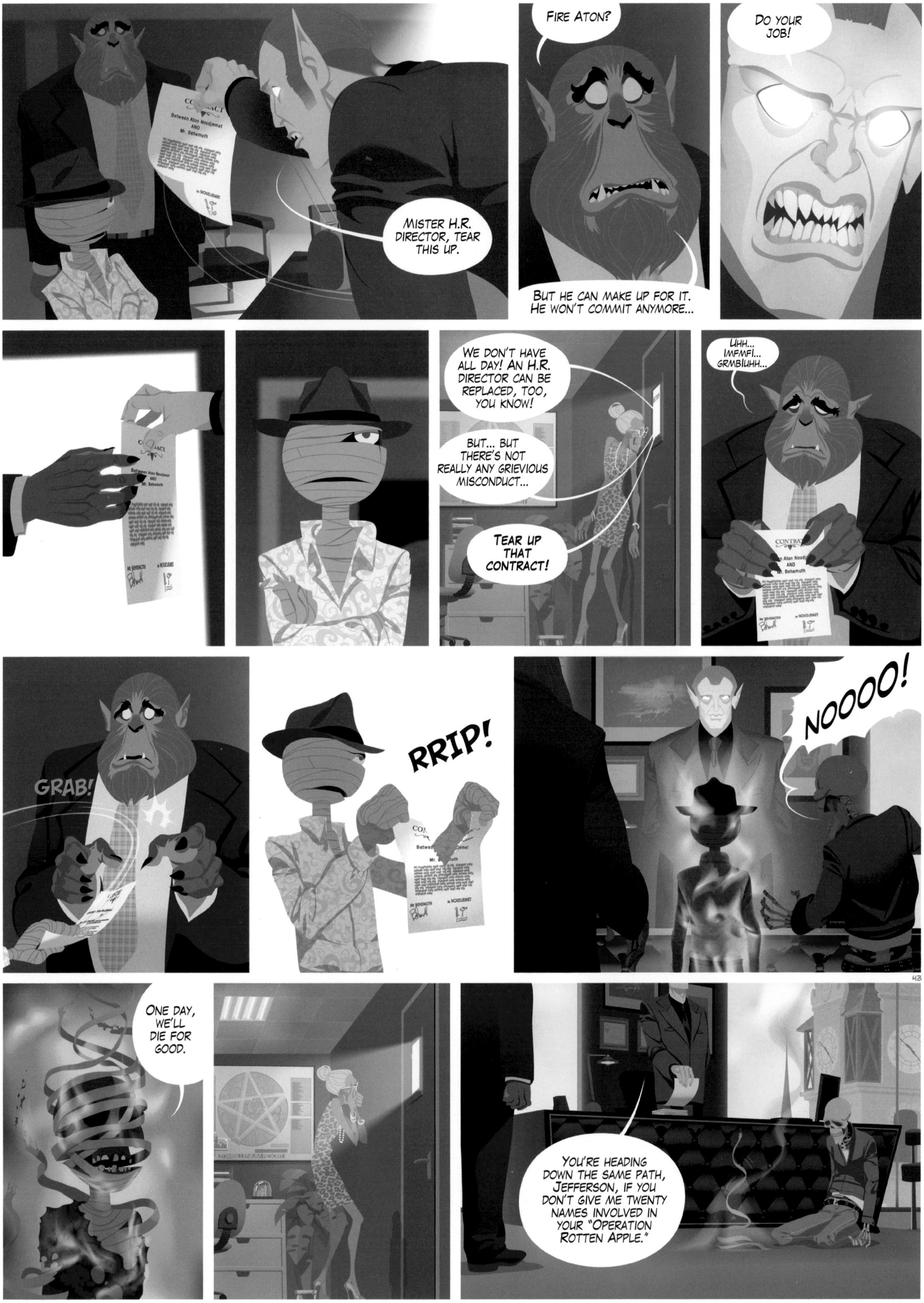
CONTRACT
Between Aton Noudjemet
AND
Mr. Behemoth
MISTER H.R. DIRECTOR, TEAR THIS UP.
FIRE ATON?
BUT HE CAN MAKE UP FOR IT. HE WON'T COMMIT ANYMORE...
DO YOUR JOB!
WE DON'T HAVE ALL DAY! AN H.R. DIRECTOR CAN BE REPLACED, TOO, YOU KNOW!
BUT... BUT THERE'S NOT REALLY ANY GRIEVIOUS MISCONDUCT...
TEAR UP THAT CONTRACT!
UHH... IMFMFI... GRMBLUHH...
GRAB!
RRIP!
NOOOO!
ONE DAY, WE'LL DIE FOR GOOD.
YOU'RE HEADING DOWN THE SAME PATH, JEFFERSON, IF YOU DON'T GIVE ME TWENTY NAMES INVOLVED IN YOUR "OPERATION ROTTEN APPLE."

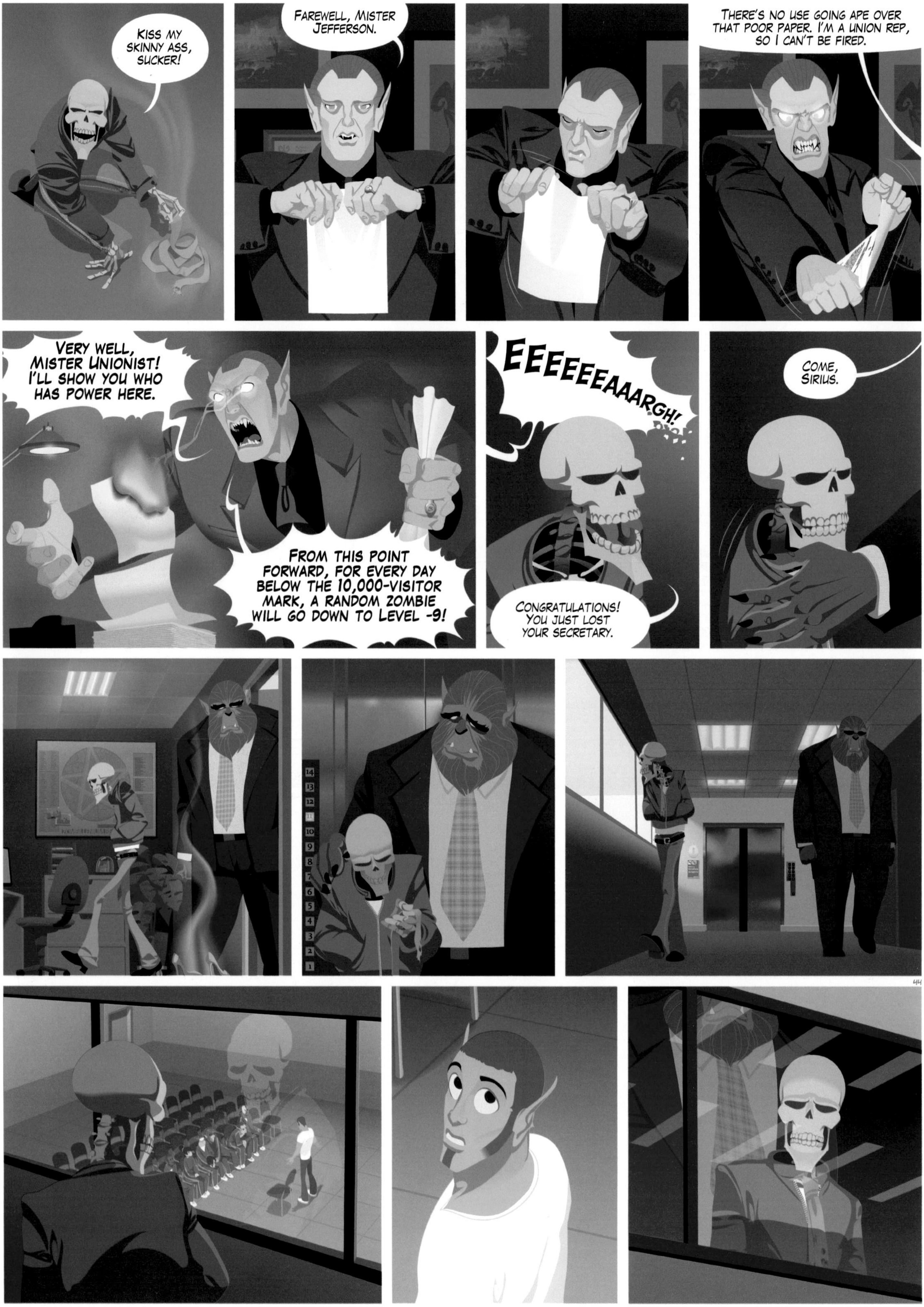
Kiss my skinny ass, sucker!
Farewell, Mister Jefferson.
There's no use going ape over that poor paper. I'm a union rep, so I can't be fired.
Very well, Mister Unionist! I'll show you who has power here.
From this point forward, for every day below the 10,000-visitor mark, a random zombie will go down to Level -9!
EEEEEEAAARGH!
Congratulations! You just lost your secretary.
Come, Sirius.

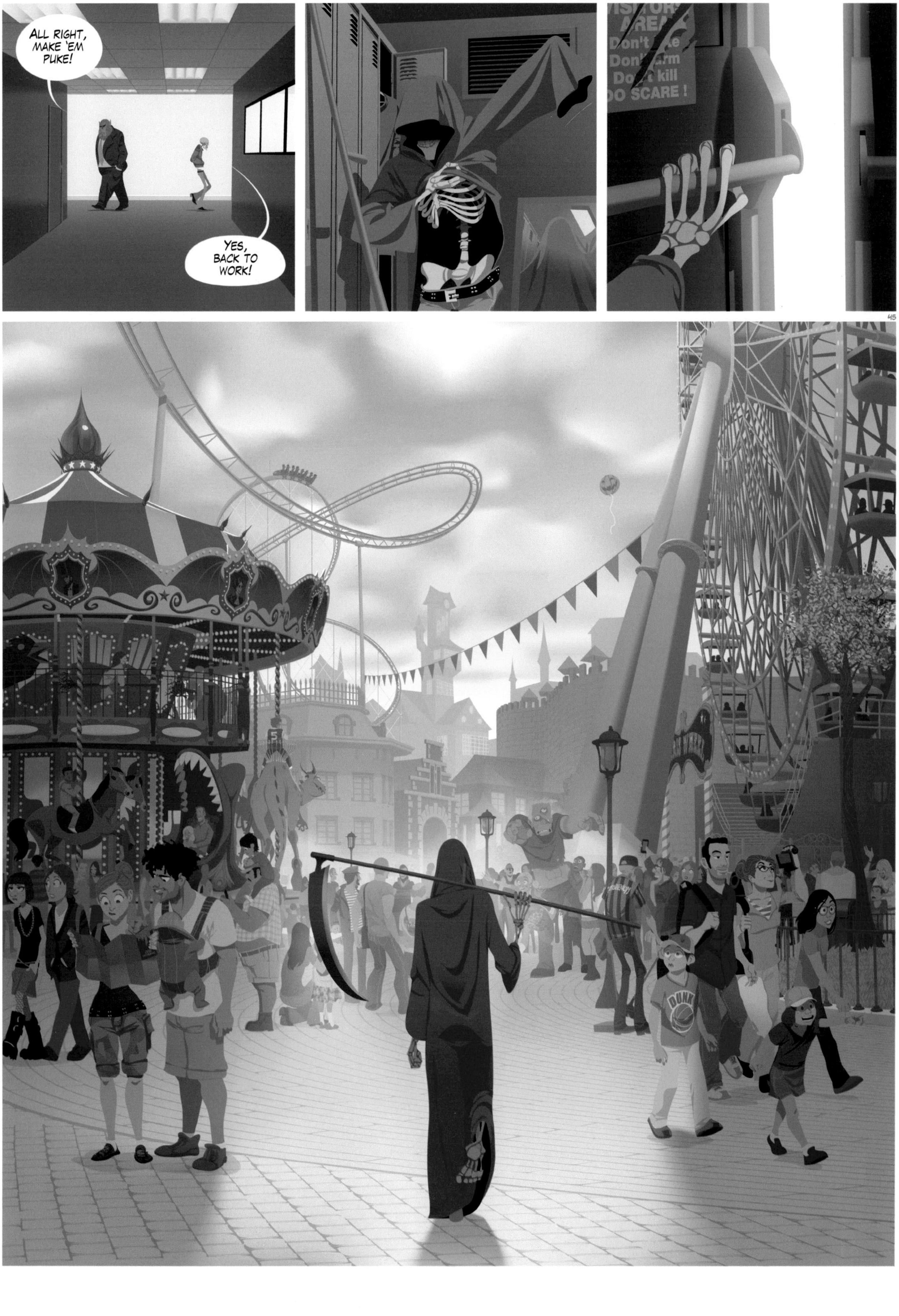
ALL RIGHT, MAKE 'EM PUKE!
YES, BACK TO WORK!
DO SCARE !

WHAT ARE YOU DOING?

AND THAT THEIR SOUL BELONGS TO THE DEVIL WHILE THEY'RE IN THE PARK. THAT'S WHY JAGGAR INSISTS ON US KILLING THEM INSIDE. AND WHY THE GUY DECAPITATED BY SIRIUS BECAME ONE OF THE LIVING DEAD.

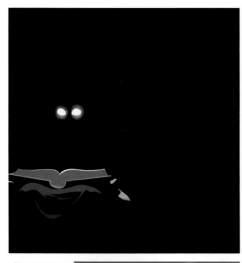

I'M READING THE COMPANY REGULATIONS.

AT THREE IN THE MORNING?

I DON'T SLEEP: I'M DEAD.

I'VE LEARNED, FOR EXAMPLE, THAT THE TICKET THE VISITORS BUY ISN'T FOR ENTRY, BUT TO EXIT.

CLAP!

DON'T YOU WANT TO TALK ABOUT SOMETHING ELSE THAN ZOMBIES?

NO, BUT WAIT, I THINK I FOUND A LOOPHOLE IN THE...

WE'LL TALK ABOUT IT AGAIN TOMORROW.

MMRRRRR

♪ TEEDEEDEEE ♫

46

IT'S FRANCIS!

HUH?

WHERE IS HE? WHAT DOES HE SAY?

HE SAYS THAT...

MY MOM SAYS HELLO.

TO BE CONTINUED

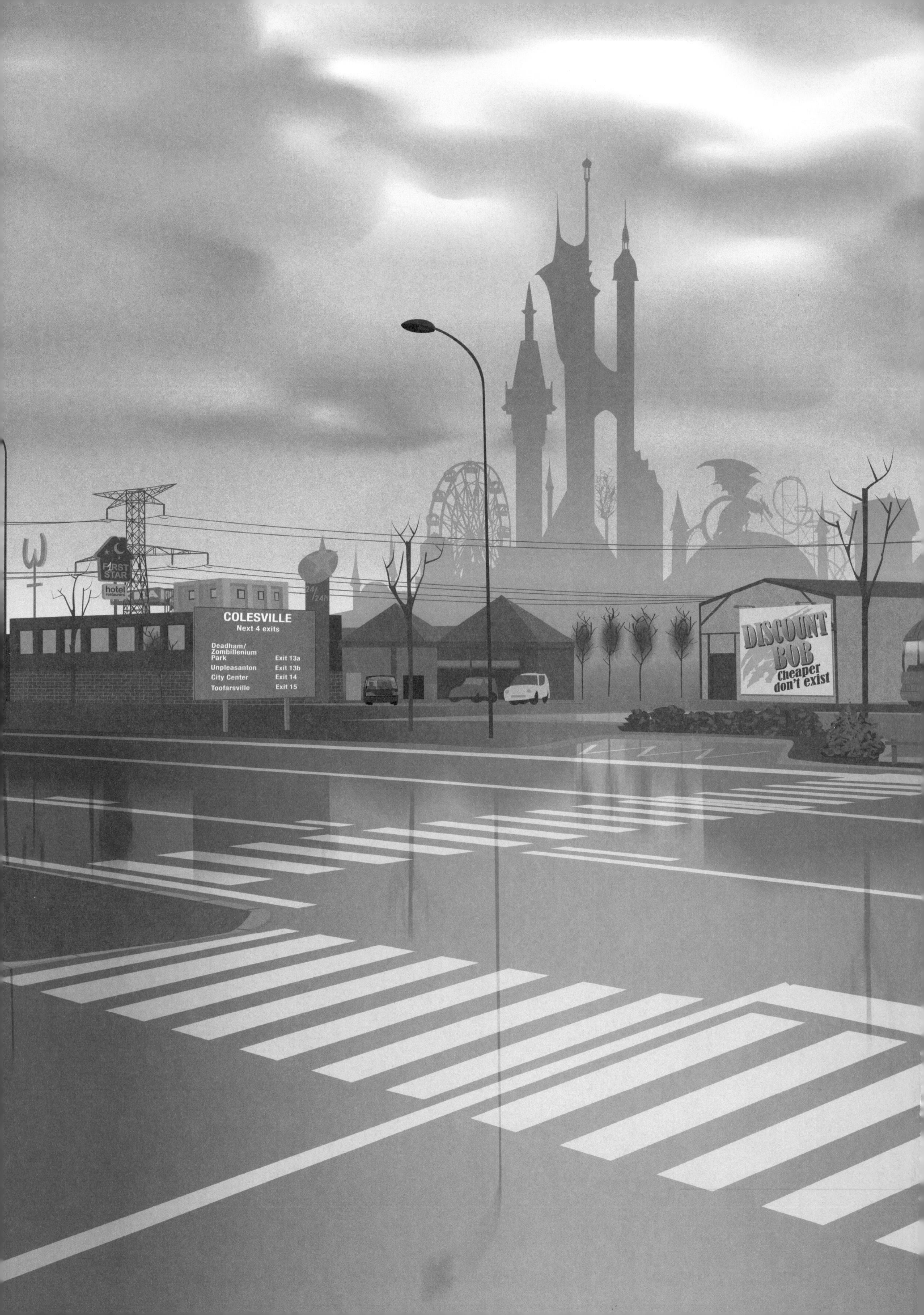

FIRST STAR
hotel
COLESVILLE
Next 4 exits
Deadham/ Zombillenium Park Exit 13a
Unpleasanton Exit 13b
City Center Exit 14
Toofarsville Exit 15
24/24
DISCOUNT BOB
Cheaper don't exist